A PRACTICAL SELF-DEFENSE GUIDE

Other books by Paul McCallum:

The Scuba Diving Handbook:
A Complete Guide to Salt and Fresh Water Diving

A PRACTICAL SELF-DEFENSE GUIDE

for women

Paul McCallum

BETTERWAY PUBLICATIONS, INC.
WHITE HALL, VIRGINIA

Published by Betterway Publications, Inc.
P.O. Box 219
Crozet, VA 22932
(804) 823-5661

Cover Design by Rick Britton
Cover photograph by Paul McCallum
Photographs by Paul McCallum
Typography by Typecasting

DISCLAIMER: The publisher and author
do not assume any responsibility for how the
information presented in this book is inter-
preted or used. The nature of martial arts
training makes injuries possible. Extreme
caution should be exercised at all times when
practicing with a partner. Readers are solely
responsible for any liability that may occur
as a result of their actions.

Library of Congress Cataloging-in-Publication Data
McCallum, Paul
    A practical self-defense guide for women /
Paul McCallum.
          p.   cm.
    Includes index.
    ISBN 1-55870-203-2 : $14.95
    1. Self-defense for women.   I. Title.
GV1111.5.M35   1991
613.6'6'082--dc20   91-4074
                                                        CIP

Printed in the United States of America
0 9 8 7 6 5 4 3 2

This Book Is Dedicated
To
Udine Way

ACKNOWLEDGMENTS

The muggers in this book who allowed themselves to be kicked, punched, kneed, jabbed, elbowed, and thrown to the ground by a variety of women... Thank you Cory Greenfield, Barry Krause, Davey "Salmo" Davis, Steve Joyner, Chipper Pastron, Jay O'Donnell, and Paul Hurst.

The women pictured in this book... Thank you Christine Lariviere McCallum, Kathleen O'Donnell, Marva Hurst, and Sharon Mulcahy.

All the excellent martial arts instructors I've been taught by over the last twenty years, most notably Dave Scully and Hawkins Cheung.

Barry Krause, for his excellent proofreading of the original manuscript.

Richard C. Schnepf, for providing me with studio space.

Glen Schnepf, for posing as a target.

Marva Hurst, for her help in the preparation of this manuscript.

Val McCallum, who attended those early classes with me and shares many of the memories...including "leg pain" in the pool.

CONTENTS

Introduction 11

1. Learning Self-Defense 13

2. Tactics 19

3. Stretching 27

4. Basic Kicks 53

5. Basic Hand Moves 67

6. In the Street 81

7. When Someone Grabs You 95

8. In Close Quarters 111

9. Sitting Down 123

10. Against a Weapon 135

11. Using Weapons 149

12. Guns 167

13. Advanced Techniques 173

14. The Aftermath 195

15. How to Pick a Martial Arts School 197

    Index 199

INTRODUCTION

Last year over 54,000 people were assaulted in Los Angeles...51,492 people were robbed, 991 people were murdered, and over 2,000 women were raped. Keep in mind that these statistics are only for *one city!* In today's society it's almost mandatory that you acquire a basic knowledge of self-defense to prevent yourself from becoming a statistic.

This book uses a unique approach to learning self-defense in that none of the women pictured is a martial artist. Experts were specifically not used to ensure that the techniques shown could truly be done by anyone — especially people with no prior self-defense training.

Self-defense works! A few days after taking the pictures of Sharon demonstrating how to use an umbrella as a weapon, Sharon herself was attacked in front of her home by a drugged-up punk who attempted to hit her over the head with a flashlight. As he ran toward her with his arm raised, Sharon "hit him in the chest with a back hand." Her assailant fell into a pile of rose bushes and then ran away!

1
LEARNING SELF-DEFENSE

Learning self-defense is *a lot easier* than you might imagine. You don't need to be in terrific physical shape, and tremendous strength is not a prerequisite to be able to defend yourself competently. In fact, relying on physical strength can be a handicap. No matter how strong you are, there is somebody in the world who is stronger.

The obvious motive to learn self-defense is to acquire the ability to overcome hoodlums, rapists, and other antagonists. But there are many other benefits to self-defense.

Exercise has become a sought-after commodity in today's society. People pay hundreds of dollars to join gyms, health clubs, and other facilities in order to stay in good physical shape. Practicing martial arts enables you to stay physically fit in addition to learning a useful skill. Hand–eye coordination is improved in addition to body coordination and muscle toning. Rather than spend boring hours doing exercises that have no practical use, *you can learn to defend yourself while getting in shape!*

SIMPLICITY

One of the most important things to remember while learning self-defense is to *keep it simple.* Under the stress of being mugged, most people find it hard to execute complicated movements that require above-average coordination. Jumping in the air and executing a spinning back kick looks terrific in the gym; trying such a maneuver in the street is difficult at best. The fact that you will be scared when under attack isn't the only reason you should stick to simple techniques. If you have to defend yourself in adverse weather, the ground may be wet or icy. You're more likely to slip while executing a difficult kick to the head than you are if you throw a simple kick to the knee.

When you work out in the gym or practice at home, you have the luxury of preparing your muscles with a series of warmup exercises. If you have to defend yourself on a cold winter night after you have been sitting at a desk all day, your muscles will be tight and stiff. If you try to execute a technique that requires flexibility or any type of physical warmup, odds are you will hurt yourself — and make your antagonist's job easier.

Keeping your techniques simple also ensures that you will remember what to do if you have to defend yourself. Kicking a belligerent punk in the groin as he tries to grab you by the throat is easy to learn, easy to execute, and easy to remember. On the other hand, a complicated series of moves such as the ones taught in some martial arts schools can be practically impossible to remember without daily practice!

So what techniques should you learn and remember? I recommend you try everything pictured in this book. You will probably find that three or four moves feel "right" physically. The Wing Chun Kick is my personal favorite. One reason for this is the fact that it feels right to me. It doesn't require any physical warmup and my body's "internal memory" retains the coordination necessary to execute this kick with tremendous power without constant practice. You will probably find a handful of kicks and punches that feel that way to you. Stick with these and perfect them. *It's much more useful to be able to execute four moves with deadly precision than to try to master everything in this book and end up being proficient at nothing!*

PRACTICE

Practice is the key to success! Once you have picked some moves that feel right to you, you need to practice them on a regular basis. There are many ways to practice martial arts.

Practice by yourself. The advantage to

practicing by yourself is you can do it anywhere at any time. Students of traditional martial arts learn "katas," which are a series of self-defense moves that make up a dance-like routine that may last for a couple of minutes. The idea is that you are fighting an imaginary opponent while performing the kata. Performing the kata enables students to practice and remember their techniques at times when no partner is available. There are no katas in this book but you can still go through the moves against an imaginary opponent. The key to success is to *really* see your opponent as you execute the moves. Imagine how he's standing, where you need to stand, and the distances involved.

If you combine your practice session with some light exercises you will find that you will give yourself a good workout!

Practice against equipment. The variety of martial arts equipment available these days is bewildering. All you really need is something to kick and something to punch. If you have a backyard or porch where a heavy punching/kicking bag can be hung, you may want to do so. There is also a wide variety of wall-mounted pads that absorb impact. The idea is that if you punch a wall at full power, you're going to hurt your hand or foot, but by putting a pad on the wall, the impact is broken while still maintaining the "feel" of hitting something solid. Combining a practice session in which you hit equipment with a "kata" session is an excellent workout.

Before attaching any equipment to walls, support posts, or overhead beams make sure that they are capable of absorbing the impact. You don't want to end up side-kicking a hole in the side of your house!

If you have a partner to help you train you can have him hold bags for you to hit. The advantage to having hand-held bags available during your workouts is that they can be held by "non-martial artists." Anyone can hold a bag for you to kick or punch.

The advantage to having somebody hold a bag is that it makes the situation more realistic. The problems of distance and timing immediately become apparent. Having the opponent move while you try to kick and punch the bag helps simulate hitting a "live" target. Hitting a moving target is harder than you might imagine and should be practiced as often as possible.

Practice with a partner. This is the ideal way to practice self-defense. Hitting bags and practicing alone are excellent ways of learning your technique, but practicing against a live opponent — especially if he has the freedom to hit back — is the best way to practice. There are three ways you can practice with a partner.

First, you can practice the techniques in a *prearranged manner*. This is often referred to as "one step" sparring. In other words, if you want to learn one of the techniques pictured in this book, you and your partner act out the scene pictured. You know exactly what he's going to do and your partner knows what your response is going to be. This type of practice is the best way to learn new techniques. You should continue practicing in this manner, in conjunction with hitting bags, until you have confidence in your ability to execute the move. Practicing these pre-rehearsed "scenes" must be done in conjunction with hitting bags. You should start out hitting slowly without power to learn the coordination involved and progress until you can strike with 100% power.

The second step is to *start sparring!* At this stage your partner has the freedom to respond in any manner he wishes. You do not know how he will attack you, nor do you know what your response will be. You may initiate the attack or wait for him to force you to defend yourself. This type of practice forces you "to think on your feet" and is an excellent way to learn about timing and distance. It also gets you used to seeing punches coming at your face, which is very important. At this stage neither you nor your partner should be hitting each other very hard. If you wish to land blows to the head, protective headgear should be worn in addition to padded gloves and padded foot gear. . .although, at this stage contact should still be light.

Another reason this type of practice is so

important is that it gets you used to being hit. Many people are terrified of being kicked or punched. Sparring allows you to experience being hit in a controlled environment and it is an excellent way to get over any fears you may have in this area. Also, sparring will give you the confidence of knowing that your techniques work.

It should be pointed out, however, that the techniques pointed out in this book are not very "sparrable." You obviously cannot kick somebody in the knee during a sparring session. Odds are you'll cripple them for life. You can, however, practice the techniques and spar with control.

Full-contact sparring should only be done by experts who have the technique to avoid injury. Complete protective gear is needed for this type of practice. As its name implies, full contact sparring is basically an all-out fight. You and your partner don protective body armor and spar...no holds barred. The idea is that this type of practice simulates the street. Full contact sparring allows you to test your skill in a setting as realistic as possible.

That said, realize that the concept of the techniques pictured in this book is based on not engaging your assailant in an all-out fight. The full-contact sparring discussed above should only be practiced by students who are enrolled in a martial arts class and have the supervision of an experienced martial arts instructor.

Wear Your Street Clothes

Initially when you're learning how to kick and punch, it's okay to wear gym clothes such as sweat pants and karate gi. However, when you are attacked, you will probably not be wearing your workout clothes. For this reason you should spend some time practicing while wearing the clothes you normally wear. One of the main considerations is the type of shoes you wear. If, for instance, your wardrobe commonly includes high heels, you should practice defending yourself with them on. Certain techniques lend themselves well to certain types of shoes and clothing, and you should practice accordingly. You will discover which techniques these are by trying to

execute them while wearing your street clothes. Obviously high kicks won't be possible while wearing tight jeans, for instance.

Practice in the Street

It's also important to practice your self-defense techniques *in the environment* you may actually have to use them! You may discover new problems when you practice in a street, garage, elevator, stairwell, or other environment. A narrow hallway, for example, may make it impossible to use kicks that require a wide radius. In that situation you would be limited to kicks and punches that travel in a straight line, such as the front kick, side kick, and Wing Chun Kick.

Practicing and thinking out what techniques will work best in really unusual places, such as on stairs and in tight quarters, is a useful way to prepare yourself for possible encounters in those situations. If some stranger were to grab you by the throat while you were walking down an isolated flight of stairs, having practiced defense in that environment previously will go a long way toward increasing your confidence and ability — and thus your chances of success.

Besides practicing in different environments you should also practice while carrying everyday items such as grocery bags, briefcases, umbrellas, books, laundry, and other items. What would you do if you had to defend your life while carrying an infant? The point is, *try to think out every possible scenario and seek a solution to it*. The techniques in this book will provide many of the answers.

BELIEVE IN YOUR ABILITY

In order to deliver your offensive with enough conviction to overcome a hoodlum who may be stronger than you and more experienced in violent exchanges, you need to *believe that your technique will work!* If you have doubts about your ability or the effectiveness of your offensive, you will not strike with enough confidence to succeed. Chances are you will also hesitate when you should not. If an antagonist senses that you are about to strike him, he will most certainly attack first.

So how do you acquire the needed confidence in your ability? Practicing the techniques you will use against a partner is an excellent confidence builder. Hitting bags, especially if they are being held by a moving opponent, is another great way to develop confidence in your skill. Imagine being hit with the blow you are throwing...if you don't feel it would hurt you, then obviously it won't hurt someone else.

One reason martial artists break boards and other items is to build confidence in the power of their blows. Although it is beyond the scope of this book to instruct you in breaking techniques, you may choose to seek instruction from a qualified instructor.

DON'T BE OVERCONFIDENT

Another potential danger with some self-defense students is that they will become overconfident after acquiring a few skills! They seek to test their newfound ability on the first person who so much as looks at them wrong. This kind of attitude can get you killed! Don't look for trouble — you'll probably find it. Street fighters have experience that you don't and you shouldn't feel capable of "challenging" someone just because you've learned a few kicks. Overconfidence is different from being confident that your techniques will work should you legitimately need to defend yourself.

It's also important to feel *morally just* in damaging someone if you are going to succeed in overcoming them. If an assailant is threatening to take your money or "bust up that pretty face," then you are justified in taking whatever action is necessary to secure your personal safety. If, on the other hand, during a movie the person sitting behind you is annoying you by talking a lot, crippling him for life is not justifiable. If you simply pick a fight you may not be able to throw yourself into battle with the necessary commitment to overcome a stronger adversary, since your actions are not justified.

VIOLENCE

One of the biggest problems faced by women learning self-defense is overcoming the conditioning induced by our society that it is socially unacceptable for women to be physically aggressive. A hoodlum who is trying to rob you of your money or life obviously doesn't care about you ...so why should you care about him? Feeling that it's wrong to hurt someone or be physically violent may inhibit you from defending yourself with the commitment necessary to succeed.

Men are raised to believe that they must defend home and family and so they don't carry the guilt some women feel about being violent. Some women actually believe they are incapable of violence; this is wrong. As a human female you have one of the strongest protective instincts of any species. A mother's maternal protectiveness is stronger than practically any other instinct. If you feel out of touch with the primal instincts necessary to defend yourself in a situation in which another person is trying to end your life, reach inside yourself, do some soul-searching, and try to tap into the primal instincts that have enabled our species to survive.

Be honest with yourself. Do you feel it is wrong for you to behave violently or hurt another individual regardless of the circumstances? If the answer is "Yes," you must find a way to come to terms with these feelings or you may fail should you have to violently defeat a potential rapist or murderer.

The other handicap some women have when it comes to martial arts is that they are squeamish about blood and the thought of breaking bones. As stated before, your attacker doesn't care about you so why should you care about him? Techniques such as jamming your thumbs into an attacker's eyes cannot be performed unless you muster the aggression required to succeed. I know it sounds "sick," but you must "want" to rip his eyes out! You must literally be in a state of mind in which you are trying to gouge his eyes out of their sockets. Understand that I am talking about a self-defense situation in which failure could mean the end of your life. How do you think a potential rapist will respond if you try to rip his eyes out and fail?

BE ECLECTIC

Keep your mind open to new sources of information and go beyond the material presented in this book. In self-defense there are no "perfect" techniques. This is one of the problems often encountered by students who limit themselves to one style of martial arts. A martial artist who is a student of a style that relies heavily on high kicks shouldn't close her mind to other techniques. For example, what if she had to defend herself while walking on an icy surface? Attempting to throw a high kick would probably only result in her slipping and complicating her situation. Conversely, this doesn't mean that high kicks are bad. The point is—keep your mind open and learn as much as you can.

YOU CAN'T LEARN JUST FROM A BOOK

The desire to acquire the knowledge to enable you to defend yourself is commendable. No one should be subject to the sick wishes of a deranged individual. Having the capability to disable a would-be antagonist will give you the confidence not to live your life in a state of fear. Buying this book was an excellent first step in learning how to defend yourself. The techniques in this book are effective and will enable you to disable a crook should the need arise. However, it is difficult to learn self-defense purely from a book. I recommend that you also enroll in a martial arts class at a reputable school for additional training. Another option is to take one of the many excellent self-defense classes offered by local police departments, colleges, YWCAs, health clubs, and some women's groups.

2
TACTICS

You're walking to your car on a dark night when suddenly two hoodlums step out of the shadows and block your path while demanding, "Give me your money!" The decisions you make in the next few seconds may determine whether you live or die! Acting scared, acting confident, immediately assaulting them, yelling, momentarily surrendering, running away — all these are just some of the options you have. One option — and probably the safest — is simply to give them what they want. Unfortunately, money may not be all that they're after. You may, in fact, be dealing with someone sadistic enough to derive his pleasure from the torment of others.

THE ADVANTAGES OF BEING A WOMAN

A mugger who attacks a woman generally expects her to be incapable of defending herself. This is a tactical advantage you shouldn't take too lightly. You don't want to give away the fact that you are capable of and ready to break his leg at the first opportunity. In the above scenario, the two assailants most definitely feel confident that they can easily overcome one woman alone in a parking lot. Imagine their reaction if you were to leap into a karate stance while yelling, "Just try me buddy!"

While in some instances this may be a good tactical choice, generally all you will be doing is alerting the attackers to the fact that they may be in for a fight. This puts their defenses on full alert and may prohibit you from landing the critical first blow. You're also giving up the important *element of surprise* that is on your side. If in the same scenario the victim acts scared and timid, cowering while saying, "Oh God, please don't hurt me...I'll give you what you want," the attackers will probably lower their defenses, feeling they have an easy prey who will not try to defend

herself. The key is to prepare to make an immediate and violent assault on your attackers while you are acting scared. An assailant moving toward a cowering woman does not expect to encounter a vicious knee-shattering side kick. An attacker who approaches a woman posed in a karate stance does.

As a woman you should never give up the element of surprise. It will always work to your advantage to make use of the fact that your attackers do not expect you to defend yourself.

However, there are no absolutes in self-defense. There may be times when asserting yourself and acting aggressively may be all that is required to stop a couple of criminals looking for an easy target.

FIRST STRIKE

You should *always* make the first move and throw the first punch or kick! If you wait for your attacker to throw the "first punch" you may get hurt and be incapable of any further defense. I know this doesn't sound very sporting, but if you wait for an attacker to throw the first blow, the element of surprise will be on his side.

Another reason that you should throw the first blow is to avoid being hit. This is extremely important! Imagine having a man punch you squarely in the face as hard as he can. The odds of your being able to "absorb" the blow and continue fighting are close to zero. Learning to block kicks and punches effectively takes a long time and requires extensive training. In order to avoid being hit, you *must throw the first punch or kick*.

SELF-DEFENSE VERSUS FIGHTING

If you have to defend yourself, you must end the confrontation as quickly as possible. The self-defense techniques in this book do not give you the skill to get involved in an all-out brawl. The goal of this type of self-defense is to injure or momentarily stun your attacker so you can then get away unharmed. You don't want to get into a situation where you're squared off with one or more assailants who are alerted to the fact that you are going to fight. If you do, the problems mentioned above of being hit come into play. A highly trained boxer has the confidence and skill to defend himself against an onslaught of vicious punches and then to turn his defense into an offense to defeat his attacker. You, on the other hand, probably do not. Remember—the key in self-defense is to *always keep the element of surprise on your side.* If an attacker is alerted to your intentions, he may block or jam your initial kick or punch, and you may not have the skill to compensate.

USING FEAR

If you are ever unfortunate enough to be in a situation in which you will have to defend yourself, you will probably be very scared. The "fight or flight" syndrome describes what happens when an animal or a human feels threatened or scared. Adrenaline rushes through your body, your heart rate dramatically increases, and you begin to sweat. All of these physiological reactions are preparing your body to either run away...or stand your ground and fight. If an attacker were to step out of a doorway and block your path, it would most likely scare you. Your heart rate would go up with a rush of adrenaline; the "fight or flight" syndrome is taking place. You need to learn to use this rush of adrenaline to carry you through the initial onslaught of an attack. It's hard to jump from a happy state of mind to a self-defensive mode in a matter of seconds. The fight or flight syndrome helps your body get physically prepared by pumping adrenaline into your system. The rush of adrenaline you get when scared can help you launch an attack against your assailant with more aggression than you thought possible.

A little mental preparation is necessary in advance. Next time something startles you, take note of how you feel and how your body reacts. Imagine having that feeling while being in a threatening situation and look for ways to release the energy rather than letting it paralyze you.

Training your body's reactions in the self-defense techniques you will use is one way to learn to release your fear when under attack. Rehearsing various scenarios you may encounter is another excellent way to prepare yourself to deal with a situation that may terrify you. If, for example, profanity offends you and being confronted by someone who yells a string of swear words scares you, then having someone say these words to you while you practice your self-defense techniques may help. You may want to get beyond the words so you can concentrate on defending yourself; the words can't hurt you, but an attacker's fist can!

MAKING NOISE

A friend of mine told me that if she were ever attacked, she would yell "Fire!" in the hopes of drawing attention to what was happening to her. In areas where people are near enough to respond, this would probably work. Screaming "Help!" on the other hand, may not draw assistance because many people become scared for their own safety and don't want to get involved.

Carrying noisemakers such as *whistles* and *compressed air horns* in your purse or pocket is an excellent idea. They can act as a deterrent before you are attacked. The idea is to make as much noise as possible before the assailant attacks you. Imagine yourself as a mugger who is following an intended victim down a dark street. Suddenly, the victim turns around and releases a continuous burst of sound from a compressed air horn. If I were a mugger in that situation, I think my reaction would be to run away before all the racket drew curious onlookers.

The potential *drawback* to using a noisemaker is that a mugger may become terrified and feel he must silence you at any cost. Generally, noisemakers are best used before you and your attacker are within "fighting range." In other words, if he's close enough to knock it out of your hand and smash you in the face, you're probably better off not using it. Once an attacker is that close to you, you must decide whether to defend yourself, run away, or give him what he wants.

Most people are aware of the screams and yells associated with martial arts practitioners. Kung Fu movies and television shows often portray practitioners flying through the air while emitting blood-thirsty screams that seem to carry on forever! Actually, *yelling* as you hit your attacker has two useful functions.

First, yelling momentarily stuns your attacker, preventing him from responding and blocking your kick or punch. Try it on a friend sometime; when he's not expecting it, yell at him and watch his reaction. He'll probably jolt from fright and freeze in his tracks for a moment. The traditional karate yell is "KI-AH!" (pronounced KEE-AH) and is said in one exhalation. The idea is to yell out the word as you strike your opponent.

Yelling psyches you up for the attack. Imagine walking out of a movie theater with your children or a friend when suddenly you are approached by a mugger who starts threatening you. As you come out of the movie, your mood is probably up, happy, and definitely not aggressive. When you are bothered by the mugger, you must instantly switch your state of mind, which can be extremely difficult to do. The fight or flight syndrome previously discussed takes care of the physiological changes that must take place, and screaming "KI-AH!" as you launch your attack helps put your mind and spirit into the necessary state required in a self-defense situation.

WHEN SHOULD YOU FIGHT?

When you are confronted by a would-be assailant, you have three choices, you can: (a) run away, (b) give him what he wants, or (c) defend yourself. You will have to evaluate the situation—sometimes in a matter of seconds—and decide which course you will take. If you feel that your

attacker intends to harm you, then obviously you must defend yourself. Generally, however, if you can get away or end the confrontation without physical force, you should do so. This has nothing to do with the morals of using physical force ...it's just that your chances of being hurt are much greater if you engage in combat.

Using violent force in a self-defense situation requires a 100% commitment from you. You cannot "test the water" by pushing or shoving an attacker to see how aggressive his response may be! If you decide to defend yourself, you must launch your attack with every intention of killing your opponent if you must. You must "want" to break his legs, to hurt him, to try to do as much physical damage to his body as possible. I know this sounds brutal but this is the state of mind you must be in to succeed. Remember, if your attacker has the opportunity to defend himself, he may kill you or do irreparable damage to your body in retaliation. If he wanted to "play fair," he wouldn't be attacking you in the first place.

If you feel incapable of carrying out this type of violent assault, then you are better off not launching any type of attack. *A halfhearted attempt may result in you failing,* and being confronted with an enraged attacker who now wants to hurt you, but who moments before would have been satisfied with your money and jewelry.

The fact that defending yourself requires such a large commitment is another reason it's better not to fight unless all other options have been exhausted.

NONVIOLENT SOLUTIONS

So...what are some nonviolent solutions?

One, you can simply comply with the mugger's wishes. If he wants your money, give it to him. If he wants your purse or jewelry, give it to him. Chances are whatever is in your purse is replaceable. Credit cards can be cancelled, a driver's license and other forms of I.D. can easily be replaced, and most of us don't carry that much cash at any given time. Giving up seventy-five dollars in cash probably isn't going to change your life at all in the long run. Losing sentimental items such as wedding rings and family jewelry is painful, but losing your life is worse and will cause your loved ones immense pain.

One problem you must keep in mind if you forfeit your identification (driver's licenses, etc.) is that the robber will know where you live. Chances are he'll simply throw your ID away and only keep the cash and saleable items he finds in your purse. If a crook gets caught with your ID on him it's not going to help prove him innocent. All the same, you should report the incident to the police and inform them that the robber may have your address.

Two, if you positively feel you cannot part with what you carry in your purse or wear on your body, then perhaps carrying some "decoy loot" may satisfy the mugger. Carrying your money and credit cards in a money belt worn under your clothes is one form of concealment. Ankle holsters, shoulder holsters, and a host of other concealable accessories can be obtained. The idea is to surrender your purse and junk jewelry in hopes of satisfying your mugger's desires. Obviously, your purse should contain ten to twenty dollars, perhaps your driver's license, and some other easily replaceable items to convince the mugger of authenticity. To prevent losing valuable jewelry, you must place it in your "concealable" carry-all prior to walking on the street or going anywhere a mugging may take place. Since people can get mugged virtually anywhere, the only real prevention is not to wear your valuables when going to questionable areas.

Three, running away is an excellent way to avoid a confrontation, especially if you can run into a public place such as a restaurant or bar. Carrying a decoy purse with you and dropping it when you flee your assailant will help ensure he won't chase you. Scream and make noise as you run—this may also help prevent the assailant from pursuing you. Realize, however, that if you are chased and caught by your assailant he will most likely try to hurt you to stop you from attempting to escape again.

So what's the solution? One option is to carry a weapon such as a gun (although not a non-violent option and you will need a carry permit to carry one *legally*). As you run away you can draw your gun...and if the mugger chases and catches you—shoot him.

You should realize, however, that shooting someone can have severe legal ramifications. You will need to convince a court that your life was in such grave danger that the use of deadly force was necessary. It is beyond the scope of this book to give advice on the legality of shooting someone, and I recommend you educate yourself on the laws that govern the area in which you live before carrying or using any type of weapon.

AVOIDING TROUBLE

The best way to avoid trouble is to make yourself an unappealing target. There are many ways to accomplish this.

Travel in a group. A person walking alone is a much more appealing target than a group of people. If you have to walk to your car every night after work, for example, try to coordinate so that you leave with some fellow workers. Something as simple as asking someone to walk you to your car may prevent you from becoming a victim. Carpooling is another excellent way to avoid being alone.

Be aware of your appearance. Imagine yourself a mugger looking for a target. You see a woman walking alone...she is dressed in expensive clothes and is wearing a large diamond ring, a gold necklace, and a bracelet, and is carrying an expensive-looking leather purse. Now imagine the same woman without the jewelry, wearing sweats and carrying an inexpensive purse. Whom would you follow and mug? I know I'm oversimplifying, but you can see the point. How you're dressed can greatly affect how appealing a target you are!

Now obviously you can't dress like a bum all the time to avoid being mugged. If you're going out to dinner with business associates or going on a date, you'll most likely want to dress up and wear your jewelry. Chances are, however, that in these situations you won't be alone and the odds of you being attacked are much less. It's unlikely you'll encounter trouble. If, however, you're going to a late movie with a girl friend it may be prudent not to get too dressed up and to leave the expensive jewelry at home.

How you dress can also affect how much of a target you become to a rapist; men can be very stimulated by what they see. When my wife wears her black miniskirt, for example, it arouses me more than when she wears loose jeans and a sweat shirt. That's normal — the miniskirt is supposed to have that effect and that's one reason she wears it. Acknowledge the fact that some clothes are sexy...and don't wear them if you're going alone to an all-night convenience store for milk.

Use common sense. Let's say you've just come home from a cocktail party but now want to go out again to rent a video. Changing out of your dress and into some "street clothes" before you go could make the difference between attracting or not attracting the attention of someone who may harm you. When heeding this advice, though, you also need to realize that rape is not considered a sexual crime, but is a violent crime. No matter how careful you are, you may still find yourself attacked by a would-be rapist.

Be aware of your environment. Here's an example of how being aware of your environment may help you avoid trouble. Let's say someone is returning to her car in an underground parking lot after a doctor's appointment. When she gets out of the elevator in the garage she looks around and notices a man standing in the shadows sixty feet away from where she's parked. Rather than take a chance on being attacked she gets back in the elevator and returns to the doctor's office where she can call the building's security guard to escort her to her car.

Because the person in the above example was aware of her environment, she spotted the possible assailant in the garage and avoided a potential confrontation. Many people walk through the day completely unaware of their surroundings. These people may walk into a bad situation they could have avoided if they had simply looked ahead. Train yourself to be over-aware of your surroundings. Take note of unusual sounds and movement and of course always keep an eye out for suspicious-looking people. The motto "Better safe than sorry" applies here.

One night I was driving home late when I came to a red light. While I was waiting for the light to change, two suspicious-looking individuals appeared out of nowhere, stepped into the street, and approached the rear right side door of my car. Since I was aware of my environment I saw them early enough to react; I ran the red light and drove through the empty intersection. Now those two guys may have been harmless...they may have also been armed and looking for someone to rob. Why stick around to find out? One of the best ways to avoid trouble is *to train yourself to see it coming so you can get out of the way.*

USING FEINTS

In a self-defense context, a feint refers to distracting your assailant's attention in order to land a kick or a punch. Feints can be verbal or physical. A physical feint could be raising your hand suddenly as if to throw a punch, thus drawing your assailant's attention up high while you simultaneously throw a kick to his groin or knee. A verbal feint is more of a distraction, such as pleading with your attacker "Please don't hurt me," in hopes of lowering his defenses, and then immediately launching an assault against him.

Think up some verbal phrases you could use to distract an attacker and lower his defenses. Rehearsing these "scenes" with a friend while practicing your self-defense techniques may be helpful. The idea is to establish your pre-assault body position while you're talking in such a way as to be in an ideal position to start your attack.

You may need to use verbal and physical distractions to enable you to move closer to an attacker before launching an assault.

Let's say, for instance, your attacker is standing ten feet in front of you and threatening to harm you if you don't give him your money. Assuming you've decided that you must defend yourself rather than give him what he wants, you will need to be much closer to him before you start your attack in order for it to be successful. Walking toward him slowly while rummaging through your purse and saying, "I'll give you what you want, just let me find my wallet" may lower his defenses long enough to allow you to get close enough to land a leg-breaking kick.

Fumbling and dropping your purse, spilling its contents all over the pavement, is another way to distract an assailant. The idea here is to put another thought or concern on his mind to confuse his thinking process the moment you attack.

Throwing something toward his face is another great way of distracting and confusing an assailant. As you walk toward him, rummaging through your purse in the manner described above, you suddenly throw something directly at his face as forcefully as you can. The idea here is that you will block his vision for a second so he can't see the kick coming toward his groin. Keys, jewelry, and other items can also be hurled at an assailant to distract him before you begin an attack.

THINK AHEAD

A little pre-planning can go a long way should you ever have to defend yourself. Imagine every possible scenario you can and think about what you would do in each situation. The self-defense techniques depicted later in this book will show you what you can do physically to defend yourself, but many other elements can also come into play. Imagine, for example, if you were lying on a beach and some stranger approached you and started making threats. Should you have to defend yourself, what is there about this environment that might aid in your defense? Well, grabbing a handful of sand and throwing it toward his face before you begin your assault might increase your chances of success. *Think about environments that you frequent.* Do you often drive late at night alone? Do you live in the city? Do you live in the country? If you examine your specific lifestyle, you may come up with some ideas that will make

defending yourself easier!

For instance, if you live alone and often have to answer the door to deliverymen and other potentially unknown people, always answering it with a can of Mace in one hand (hidden from view) would certainly enhance your chances of success should you have to launch an attack.

The point is, think about what you will do in various situations while you are sitting in the safety of your home. The techniques described in this book are only one side of the coin — your brain is the other.

WHERE TO HIT

Knowing where to hit your opponent is important; here's a list of targets on the human body.

A) **Forehead.** Hitting your opponent on the forehead will stun him or even knock him out if you hit hard enough. A Palm Strike is an excellent technique to use; Elbow Strikes and Front Punches are also good weapons to hit the forehead with.

B) **Temple.** A blow to the temple can kill. A variety of hand strikes can be used, with the Ridge Hand being one of the most effective. You can also strike the temple with your Elbow or Backfist.

C) **Eyes.** Attacking someone's eyes can affect them psychologically as well as physically. A Finger Jab can be used to attack them.

D) **Nose.** If you hit someone's nose, you will probably break it. A broken nose is extremely painful and causes your opponent's eyes to swell up, making it hard for him to see.

E) **Mouth.** I recommend you avoid the mouth as target. While you will do damage to your opponent, you may also do damage to your hand on his teeth. Aim a little higher and hit him in the nose.

F) **Chin.** A blow to the chin can knock your opponent out. The idea is to "snap" his head backward. Palm Strikes, Punches, and Elbow Strikes are all good techniques to use.

G) **Neck.** Hitting someone in the front of the neck can kill them. A variety of Chopping techniques can be used. The Ridge Hand is also a good

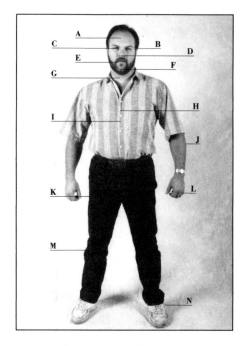

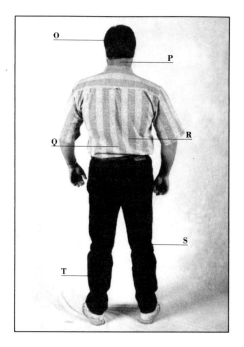

weapon to hit the neck with.

H) **Sternum.** Commonly called the breast bone, the sternum is another target where a hard strike can kill. If you hit hard enough the bone will shatter, sending bone splinters into the heart. A Straight Punch and a Palm Strike are both good hand strikes to use. A knee to the sternum is also effective.

I) **Solar Plexus.** This region of sensitive nerves just below the sternum is an excellent target. A Straight Punch and a Palm Strike are good hand blows to use. Front, Round, and Side Kicks are also effective, as are Knee Strikes.

J) **Elbow.** The elbow is targeted when you want to break the arm. A variety of Armlocks can be used.

K) **Groin.** Not much needs to be said here except kick him hard!

L) **Fingers.** If your opponent's hands are open, kick or punch into his fingers. A broken finger hurts — it also helps stop him from punching you. If you "take away his weapons" he can't hurt you.

M) **Knee.** If he can't walk he can't fight! A kick to the knee is painful at the least . . . and a broken leg is incapacitating. The Side Kick and the Wing

Chun Kick are both excellent weapons to hit the knee with.

N) **Foot.** If you're wearing hard shoes a kick or "stomp" to your opponent's foot can be effective. At the very least it will draw his attention down as you set him up for a punch to the face.

O) **Back of the Head.** Hitting someone in this area can knock him out. The idea is to "snap" his head forward when you strike. A Palm Strike is a good choice here.

P) **Back of the Neck.** A hard hit here can break the neck. A variety of "chopping" techniques can be used. Hitting to this area is a common follow-up blow after you have kicked or kneed him in the groin, making him bend over.

Q) **Kidneys.** Hitting someone in the kidneys can incapacitate him. A hit to the kidneys can also do lasting damage or even kill; a variety of kicks and punches can be used.

S) **Back of the Knee.** Hitting to this area will force your opponent's leg to bend forward, throwing him off balance.

T) **Calf.** Used as a target when you want to "sweep" your opponent's leg out from under him.

3
STRETCHING

The majority of kicks in this book do not require extensive limberness. In fact, most of the techniques demonstrated were picked because they can be done without any type of warmup—since the odds of your being warmed up and stretched out at the moment you are attacked are slim.

It's a good idea, however, to *warm up your muscles anytime you are going to engage in physical activity,* especially when you're going to do a continuous exercise such as kicking. If you have to defend yourself you may only throw one kick, but you may throw fifty kicks in a practice session. Stretching loosens and warms up your muscles, making it easier to execute the new movements you are learning.

Don't feel you have to do all the exercises pictured; pick a few that you like and just use those. The exercises in this chapter cover a wide range of skill levels ranging from novice to advanced, so there should be something for everyone.

When stretching remember these four things:
Don't force a stretch. Stretching should be done in a relaxed manner. Simply exhale and gently lean into the stretch as far as you can comfortably go—and then hold that position as you breathe deeply. All movements should be slow and relaxed. Under no circumstances should you try to "bounce" yourself lower into a stretch.

Remember to breathe! Many people hold their breath when they stretch—which obviously isn't good. Exhale as you lean into a stretch and then continue to take deep slow breaths as you hold it and relax. If you find your breathing becoming fast or strained while stretching, you're probably overdoing it.

Start slow and easy. Always begin your stretching sessions with easy exercises such as neck, wrist, and ankle rolls before you proceed to the more difficult exercises. Give your body a chance to "warm up for the warmup."

If you feel pain stop! Listen to what your body is telling you. If an exercise makes your back hurt, for example, don't do it.

Head Roll and Neck Stretch

1. Stand upright with your feet about shoulder-width apart.

2. Roll your head to the right.

3. Move your head in a circular motion to the back.

4. Continue the circle rolling to the left.

5. Roll to the front. After you've done a few head rolls in one direction, reverse and roll your head the other way.

6. To get a better stretch along the back of your neck, place your hands on the back of your head and gently pull your head forward.

Shoulder Roll

7. Stand in an upright position and roll your shoulders in a circle. Start by moving them upward.

8. Roll your shoulders back...then down.

9. Complete the circle by moving them forward. After you've done a few circles, reverse direction and roll the other way.

Arm Rolls

10. Start with your arms extended out in front of you.

11. Swing your arms forward and up in a circle, keeping them extended.

12. Continue the circle, swinging your arms behind you. It's okay for your arms to move farther apart when they're behind your back.

13. Continue rolling your arms to complete the circle. After you've done a few circles in one direction, reverse and roll your arms the other way.

Shoulder and Arm Stretch # 1

14. Extend your right arm and take hold of your elbow as pictured.

15. Pull the arm across your body to the left. Repeat the exercise with the opposite arm.

Shoulder and Arm Stretch # 2

16. Extend your left arm over your head and grab your elbow with the opposite arm as pictured.

17. Bend your left arm and gently pull the arm to the right with your opposite hand. Repeat the exercise with your other arm.

Ankle Stretch # 1

18. Sit on the floor with your legs extended in front of you. Pull your toes toward you.

19. Point your toes.

Ankle Stretch # 2

20. Sit on the floor and bend your right leg across your left.

21. Roll your ankle in a circle. Reverse direction of the circle.

Back, Leg and Arm Stretch

This is an advanced stretch. You may find that a few inches of movement is all that is required before you feel a stretch.

22. Stand with your feet about shoulder-width apart and lace your fingers behind your back.

23. Keeping your back straight, start to bend forward. Lift your head up as you bend.

24. For a more advanced stretch, bend farther forward and extend your arms into the air behind your back.

25. Relax your head and neck and bend completely forward. Let the weight of your arms stretch them over your head.

Waist Stretch

26. Start in an upright position and lean your upper body to the right. Keep your hands on your hips. You should feel a stretch along the left side of your torso.

27. Lean to the left, stretching the right side of your torso.

28. Lean forward, stretching your legs and back. Remember to keep your back straight and your head up.

29. Keep your hands on your hips and start to lean back.

30. Relax your head and let it fall backward. If you are new to stretching, don't continue this exercise beyond this point.

31. For an advanced stretch, extend your arms over your head and lean your shoulders back.

Side Stretch

32. Another alternative is to place your hands on your hips. This stretch should not be attempted by beginners.

33. With your feet about shoulder-width apart, raise your left arm over your head and stretch to the right. Place your right arm on your hip or leg to help support your body.

34. Repeat the exercise in the other direction.

Inner Thigh Stretch

35. Stand with your legs a few feet apart and bend your right leg while keeping the opposite leg straight. Keep your feet flat on the floor, hands on your hips.

36. Repeat the exercise in the other direction. Alternate between left and right a few times.

37. Adding your hands to the stretch makes the exercise more advanced. Reach behind your bent right leg with your left hand. Extend your free hand into the air.

38. Rotate to the other side and repeat the exercise.

Wrist and Forearm Stretch

39. Kneel on the floor and place your palms on the floor, fingers pointing toward your knees. Don't apply full pressure if your forearms feel tight.

40. Turn your fingers inward.

41. Turn one hand forward and one back...and then switch hand positions.

Push-Ups

42. Rest your weight on your knees and hands as shown.

43. Bend your arms and lower yourself to the floor. Don't let your head collapse to the floor and remember to keep your back straight. Extend your arms and return to the starting position. Try to do ten repetitions.

44. Another variation is to do the push-ups with your fingers turned inward.

45. Lower yourself to the floor, but don't allow your chest to actually touch. Extend your arms and return to the starting position.

Calf Stretch

46. Place your hands on the floor as shown and raise the heels of your feet off the ground.

47. Lower your heels to the floor, stretching your calf muscles.

Stomach Stretch

48. Kneel on the floor with your hands on the ground in front of you.

49. Slide your hands forward, stretching your stomach. Don't let your butt or legs move forward. Your arms will also get a stretch with this exercise.

Leg Stretch

50. Kneel on one leg while extending the other straight in front of you. For some people this position may provide enough stretch. If your leg feels tight, don't overdo it. You can provide a little extra stretch if desired by simply leaning a few inches forward.

51. For an intermediate stretch, place your hands on either side of your leg and bend forward, keeping your back straight as you go.

52. For an advanced stretch, lower your head to your knee and place your forearms on the ground on each side of your leg.

53. Repeat the exercise with the other leg.

54. Intermediate stretch.

55. Advanced stretch.

Inner Leg Stretch

56. Sit on the floor and place the soles of your feet together as shown. Grab your feet with your hands and pull them toward you.

57. Lower your head to your feet.

Full Thigh Stretch

58. Raise your head and shoulders (from position #57) and start to extend your feet out in front of you. For a full stretch, keep your hands on your ankles. For a less strenuous stretch, do not hold your ankles while you extend your legs.

59. Straighten your legs and lower your chest to your thighs. Keep your head up. For an intermediate stretch, keep your hands on your ankles as shown. If your legs feel tight, simply lean forward with your hands on the floor beside you.

Straddle Stretch

60. With your hands resting on your ankles, lower your head to your knees. Remember to keep your back straight.

61. Keep your hands on your ankles and raise your head off your knees. To make the stretch easier, raise your torso to a more upright position and place your hands on your thighs.

62. Open your legs to the side. If leaning over them creates too much of a stretch, keep your torso upright.

63. For an advanced stretch, continue to open your legs until they are extended to the side.

Back Stretch

64. Sit on your butt with your hands placed behind you as pictured.

65. Place your left arm along the right side of your right leg and gently twist your upper body to the right.

66. Repeat the exercise on the other side of your body.

Back and Leg Stretch

67. The above stretch can be made more difficult by adjusting your position as shown.

68. Place your left arm on the right side of your right knee and gently twist your body to the right.

69. Return to the starting position and then reverse the position of your legs.

70. Repeat the exercise on the other side of your body.

Waist Stretch

71. Lie on your back with your arms extended out to the side.

72. Bend both knees.

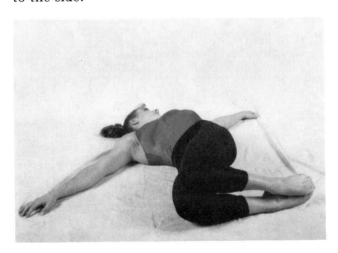

73. Twist your knees to the right and lower them to the floor while you keep both shoulders on the ground and look to the left.

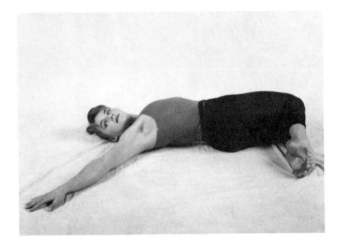

74. Repeat the exercise on the other side of your body.

Hip Stretch

75. Lie on your back and raise your left knee to your chest. Hold it there with both hands.

76. Lower your knee to the right, guiding it with your right hand. Your left arm should be extended to the side.

77. Return your leg to the center position and raise the other knee.

78. Repeat the exercise on the other side of your body.

Sit-Ups

Caution: You should not do sit-ups if you have a weak lower back.

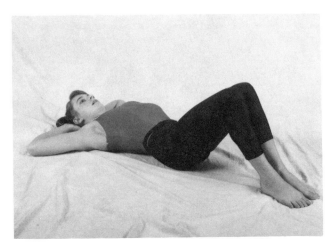

79. Lie on your back with your hands behind your head and your knees bent.

80. Raise your shoulders off the ground by tightening your stomach muscles. Do not "lift" your head with your hands. Keep your lower back on the ground.

Advanced Sit-Ups

81. Lie on the floor with your hands behind your head, your knees bent and your feet raised off the floor, and your legs crossed at the ankles.

82. Raise your shoulders off the ground by tightening your stomach. Keep your lower back on the ground.

Side Sit-Ups

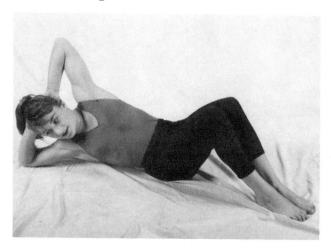

83. Lie on the floor as shown in # 79. Twist to the right, raising your shoulders and back off the ground. This is an advanced exercise.

84. Repeat the exercise on the other side of your body.

The Bridge

This back bend helps stretch and loosen up your back.

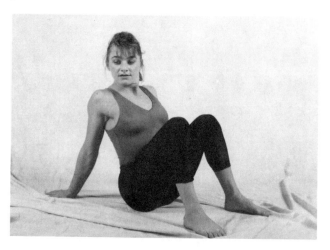

85. Start in a sitting position with your hands behind your back.

86. Straighten your arms and legs and arch your back off the floor. Lower yourself down gently.

Runner's Stretch

87. Extend your left leg to the side and bend your right leg behind you.

88. Lift your left arm and reach over your head to the right. You will feel a stretch along the left side of your body.

89. Grab your left ankle with your left hand while keeping your back straight. If you can't reach your ankle, hold your thigh or knee instead. You will feel a stretch along your "hamstring."

90. For an advanced stretch, raise your right arm over your head and grab your left ankle.

91. Place both hands on your ankle and lower your head to your leg while keeping your back straight.

92. Return to an upright position.

93. Place your hands in front of your body and start to slide them out...stop when you feel a stretch.

94. For an advanced stretch, slide your hands forward until your chest is resting on the ground.

Advanced Leg Stretch

95. Place your hands on the floor and slide your feet out to the side.

96. Continue to slide your feet apart.

97. Keep your back straight and lower your butt to the ground.

98. Raise your left arm over your head and grab your right ankle.

99. Repeat the exercise on the other side of your body.

100. Keep your legs to the side and lower your chest to the floor.

4
BASIC KICKS

The kicks demonstrated in this chapter are used throughout the rest of the book. You can either begin with this chapter and learn how to do the kicks first...or you can use this chapter as a reference as you read through the book and encounter kicks you don't know how to do.

If you can, practice in front of a full-length mirror. That way as you learn you can compare your reflection with the pictures. Working out with a partner is also helpful; have them hold the book and compare your form with the pictures.

Don't try to kick with any power or speed at first. Spend time doing the moves slowly until you begin to "feel" them. It's better to be relaxed when you're learning new moves than to be tight and tense. *Concentrate on your form at first, not power;* once you have the proper form, power will come naturally.

Kicking high is not important. In fact, in a self-defense situation your kicks will usually be aimed at your opponent's knee or groin. Also, to deliver a high kick you'll have to stretch first — a luxury a mugger probably won't allow you in the moments before he attacks!

Warm up with some stretching exercises before each practice session. If a kick movement feels "tight," don't force it. Either do the movement lower and slower or go back and do some additional warmup exercises.

It's not necessary for you to learn all the kicks pictured. If you find certain kicks hard to execute or simply don't like a kick, don't bother with it. Concentrate on the kicks that you like. If a kick is hard to do in practice, it may be impossible to do under the stress of being mugged. Remember, it's better to be able to do three kicks well than ten poorly!

Basic Stance

1. This is a basic fighting stance. It is referred to as a "left side forward" stance because the left foot and hand are in front. A "right side forward" stance would have the right leg and arm in front. Feet should be a little wider than shoulder-width apart, with your weight distributed about equally on each foot. Hands should be held at the ready with fists closed.

The fighting stance should be used while you are learning. In the street, however, it may be a mistake to leap into a fighting stance since doing so will alert your opponent as to your intentions. You can stand in a "relaxed" fighting stance by standing sideways to your opponent with your hands at the sides. This way you will be ready to defend yourself should there be a need...but you won't look like you're inviting a fight.

Front Kick

2. Start in a "left side forward" fighting stance.

3. Move your rear leg forward and begin to raise your knee.

4. Lift your knee up in preparation to throw the kick. One way to do it is to aim your knee at the intended target.

5. Extend your leg and kick. Contact can be made with either the ball or instep of your foot.

Front Knee Kick

6. Start in a fighting stance.

7. Bring your rear leg forward and raise your knee as if to throw a front kick.

Side Kick

8. Continue to raise your knee into the target.

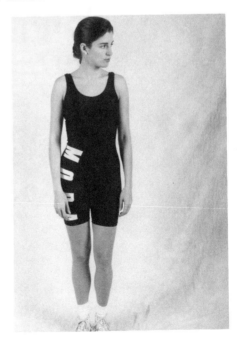

9. This kick can be thrown from a normal standing position, which gives your attacker almost no warning as to your intent.

10. Raise your knee.

11. "Stomp" your heel out at your opponent's knee.

12. Here's how the kick looks from the opponent's perspective. Also note that when you stand sideways you present less of a target.

13. Raise your knee.

14. "Stomp" your heel out at your opponent's knee.

Moving Forward Side Kick

15. This is a way of throwing a side kick at an opponent who is a little farther away from you. Start in a fighting stance.

16. Move your rear leg forward and cross it behind your front leg.

17. Raise your front knee and prepare to kick.

18. Drive your foot out sideways at your opponent.

19. Looking at the moving forward side kick from the side — start in a fighting stance.

20. Bring your rear leg forward and cross it behind your front leg.

21. Raise your knee in preparation to kick.

22. Drive your leg out sideways. Pull your toes back and try to make contact with the heel of your foot.

Crescent Kick

23. This kick lets you kick around an opponent's front leg so you can reach his groin. Start in a "left side forward" fighting stance.

24. Raise your front leg and move your ankle to the right. The idea is to have your ankle farther to the right than the knee of the same leg.

25. Kick your toes out...and from right to left into your opponent's groin.

26. Looking at the crescent kick from the front, your end position should look like this.

Hook Kick

27. This kick is often used as "a leg sweep." Start in a fighting stance.

28. Move your rear leg forward and then extend your front leg as pictured. Pull your toes back and prepare to "sweep" with your heel.

29. "Hook" your opponent's leg by bending your knee and pulling his leg slightly toward you.

Round Knee Kick

30. Start in a fighting stance.

31. Bring the knee of your rear leg forward and let your foot drift out to the side slightly.

Front Leg Round Kick

32. Drive your knee into your opponent's rib cage.

33. Start in a fighting stance.

34. Move your rear leg forward until it almost touches your front leg.

35. Raise your front knee with your ankle to the side.

Rear Leg Round Kick

36. Extend your leg and kick with your instep, the ball of your foot, or your shin.

37. Start in a fighting stance.

38. Bring your rear knee forward...

39. ...and prepare to throw a round kick by moving your ankle and shin to the side of your body.

40. Extend your leg...

41. ...and kick.

Spin Kick

42. Start in a left side forward fighting stance.

43. Pivot on your front foot, turn to your right (backward), and lift your right knee in preparation to kick.

44. Continue to spin.

45. Drive the heel of your foot out in the same manner as a side kick. In essence a spin kick is a backward turning side kick.

Wing Chun Kick

46. Start in a left side forward fighting stance.

47. Raise your front knee...

48. ...turn your toes to the left and "stomp" your opponent's knee.

5
BASIC HAND MOVES

The punches and hand movements demonstrated in this chapter are used throughout the rest of the book. Spend some time with this chapter to get a feel for these basics. Learning the individual moves one at a time is a lot easier than immediately trying to execute techniques that require a combination of kicks and punches.

As with the previous chapter, practicing in front of a mirror will be beneficial since you'll be able to compare your form with the pictures.

Practice in "slow motion" at first — until you can do the moves without referring to the text. Then increase speed, but not power. If you try to hit with force before your form is correct, your body will learn bad habits that will be hard to eliminate later.

As with all the techniques in this book, practice them with both sides of your body.

Front Punch

This is one of the simplest self-defense techniques. It's also one of the most effective. This punch can be thrown fast since it only has to travel about two feet before it reaches your opponent's face. If you are standing in front of your opponent with your hands resting on your lapel before you throw the punch/punches, the chances of him being able to react quickly enough to block you are almost nonexistent.

1. Hold your left hand in front of you as if you had just thrown a punch as pictured. Do not let your elbow "drift" out to the side. Keep the arm straight with a little bend at the elbow joint... avoid "locking your arm."

2. Begin to pull your left hand toward your chest as you simultaneously start to "punch" your right hand out. The right hand will pass over the top of your left. Both hands travel along an imagined "center line" in front of your body.

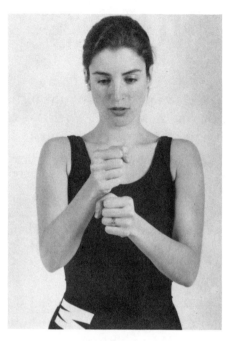

3. Continue to pull your left hand back while you drive your right hand forward. Remember that the punching hand passes over the top of the hand that's being withdrawn.

4. Punch straight out with your right hand.

5. Side view of the left front punch. Note the slight bend at the elbow.

6. Pull back the right hand as the left hand moves forward to punch. Remember that both hands travel in a straight line and that the punching hand passes over the top of the hand that's being withdrawn.

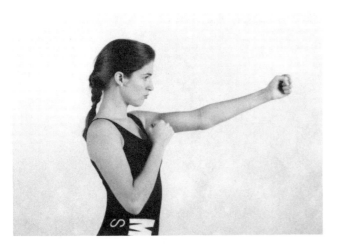

7. Punch with your left hand.

Ridge Hand

This is an extremely powerful blow. The key to generating power is to rotate your shoulder forward as you swing your arm. The "feel" is similar to swinging a rock on the end of a piece of rope, your arm being the rope and your hand the rock. You can easily knock a man out with this strike.

8. Stand in a left side forward fighting stance and extend your right arm behind you.

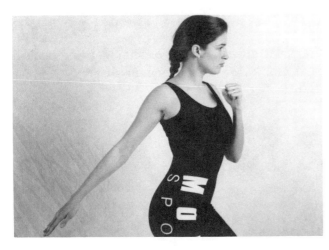

9. A side view of your right arm held in preparation.

10. Move your right shoulder and upper body forward and let your stiff arm travel forward too.

11. Continue the forward motion and strike your opponent in the head with the inside ridge of your hand. It's important to remember to tuck your thumb under the palm of your hand to avoid breaking your thumb.

Horizontal Elbow

12. With your left side forward, hold your right elbow bent behind you as pictured.

13. Swing your shoulders and hips to the left and let your elbow move forward on a horizontal plane.

14. Continue rotating your shoulders and smash your elbow into your opponent's face.

Vertical Elbow

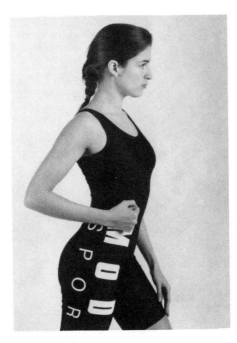

15. Hold your right fist at your side, bending your elbow behind you.

16. Move your elbow forward.

17. Drive your elbow forward and upward in a vertical plane.

18. Smash your elbow into your opponent's face.

19. Withdraw your right elbow as you simultaneously bring your left elbow forward in preparation to strike.

20. Drive your left elbow into your opponent's face.

21. A front view of the left elbow being withdrawn as the right elbow prepares to strike.

22. Drive the right elbow into your opponent's face.

Elbow Jab

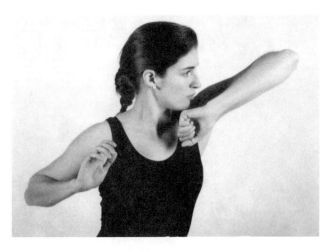

23. Bend your arm in front of your chest as pictured. The key is to move the fist of your front hand toward your rear shoulder as you prepare to strike.

24. Drive your elbow into your opponent's face.

Backfist

25. Stand "left side forward" as pictured. The idea is to hold your hands high enough to defend yourself if you need to, but not high enough to alert your attacker to your intentions.

26. Without any warning begin to extend your front fist forward.

27. Continue to unfold your arm.

28. Strike your opponent in the face with the back of your fist.

Karate Chop

29. Assume a left side forward fighting stance and raise your right hand behind your head as pictured.

30. Swing your hand forward in a "chopping" motion. The key to generating power is to rotate your shoulders with the arm.

31. "Chop" your opponent in the neck.

32. A left hand karate chop about to be thrown, viewed from the front.

33. Note the difference in shoulder position once the blow has landed.

34. Right hand karate chop about to be thrown.

35. Note the difference in shoulder position once the blow has landed.

Blocks

As a general rule men possess more physical strength than women. If someone stronger than yourself is trying to punch you it makes a lot more sense to get out of the way of the blow than to try to meet it head-on.

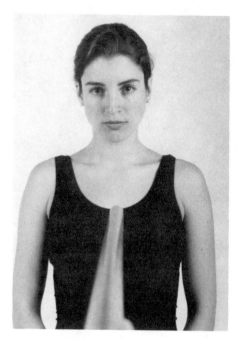

36. The staff represents an attack coming straight at you.

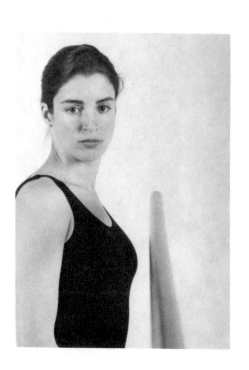

37. As the staff (or punch) moves forward shift your body to the right. The idea is that even if you miss blocking the attack, your body will not have to absorb the entire strike since you have moved out of the way.

38. As you move to the side, block the attack with the palm of your hand.

39. You could also shift your body to the left.

40. Simultaneously block the attack with the palm of your hand.

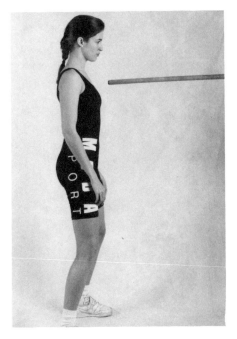

41. Facing an incoming assault.

42. Shift your body to the left and block the attack.

Palm Strike

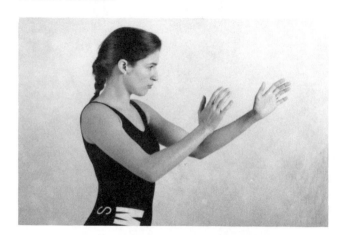

43. Hold your hands in an open-handed "guard" position.

44. Drive the palm of your right hand into your opponent's face. Note the difference in shoulder position.

45. Withdraw the right hand as you simultaneously move your left hand forward to strike.

46. Drive the palm of your left hand into your opponent's face.

47. Raise your hands to indicate that you do not intend to fight; this is a great "sucker punch." All you have to do is rotate your shoulder forward and extend your palm into his face. With a little practice this move can be made with great speed and power.

48. Suddenly drive the heel of your hand into your opponent's face.

Achieving Maximum Power

The key to producing power when you hit is to turn your hips, upper body, and shoulders into the blow. Here's an exercise to help develop the needed coordination.

49. Stand with your feet about shoulder-width apart and your elbow held out in front of you.

50. Start to swing your left shoulder and elbow forward as you pull the right one back.

51. Continue to rotate until your left elbow is in front.

52. Here's the same exercise as viewed from the side.

53. Turn your waist and shoulders.

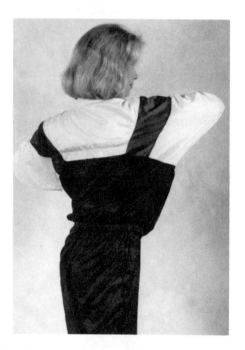

54. Continue turning until your opposite elbow is forward.

After you start to get a feel for this exercise, try doing it with different hand moves such as palm strikes and front punches.

6
IN THE STREET

In this chapter you will begin to take the basic kicks and punches learned in the previous chapters and apply them in various self-defense situations. When practicing, remember to try the techniques with *both sides of your body*. A real attacker may not reach with his left hand, and you don't want to be "handicapped" by the fact that you never practiced kicking with your right foot.

While learning these techniques, move slowly at first until you work out the distances involved. "Timing" is the key to success. If you throw a punch or kick too early, you'll miss your oppo-

nent; throw it too late, and he may "jam" or block you. Another reason to move slowly is to avoid hurting your training partner. As a beginner you may not have the physical control needed to avoid hurting someone.

After you've gained an understanding of the moves involved, have your partner hold a bag for you to kick or a "mitt" for you to punch so that you can try the techniques at "full power." You can buy this type of equipment at a local sporting goods or martial arts store.

Front Kick

1. You are approached by a robber who demands that you give him money or he will hurt you.

2. Step toward him with your left foot and deliver a front kick to his groin with your right foot.

Spin Kick # 1

3. A mugger approaches you, so you assume a right side forward stance.

4. As he moves toward you, shift your weight to your right leg and start to spin to your left as you raise your left leg and prepare to kick.

5. Continue to spin, building up speed and momentum. Keep your knee up as you come round.

6. Kick him in the stomach.

Spin Kick # 2

The spin kick can sometimes be used effectively if you're caught off guard.

7. While talking on a public phone you are harassed by a hoodlum.

8. As he moves toward you, drop the phone and prepare to spin kick.

9. Spin to your left, raising your left foot as you go in preparation to kick.

10. Kick him in the stomach.

Palm Strike

This is an easy way to hit someone fast.

11. A mugger is threatening you.

12. As he reaches out to grab you, knock his hand away from your body with a "wiping" motion. Keep the palm of your hand facing him.

13. Immediately follow up with a palm strike to his head.

14. Remember to twist your shoulder into the blow and to follow through.

Side Kick

A side kick to the knee is one of the fastest ways to end an unwanted confrontation. If you kick with enough force you will break your opponent's leg...if he can't walk he can't pursue you any farther.

15. A man threatens to punch you.

16. Lean way back to avoid being hit with the punch.

17. At the same instant side kick him in the knee.

18. It doesn't take much power to break your opponent's leg with this kick.

Front Punch

The shortest distance between two points is a straight line. In other words, the fastest way to hit someone is to punch him straight in the face!

19. A thug is threatening you.

20. Suddenly he reaches out to grab you.

21. Step forward with your left leg and throw a straight left punch to his face.

22. Immediately follow up with a right straight punch to his face.

High Feint / Front Punch

23. You are being harassed by someone who is threatening to harm you.

24. Suddenly step forward with your right leg as you simultaneously throw a finger jab at his eyes. You want him to block your finger jab, so throwing it a little short of his face may help ensure he reacts as desired.

25. When he blocks your finger jab...

26. ...grab his wrist.

Slap Block / Punch

27. Pull his wrist toward your body with your right hand while you simultaneously throw a left straight punch into his face.

28. A mugger approaches you.

29. Suddenly he reaches out to push or punch you.

30. As his hand approaches, you slap it to the side with your right hand and at the same time throw a straight punch at his head.

31. Maintain control of his arm as you hit him.

Front Kick / Ridge Hand

32. A man is threatening you.

33. Front kick his groin with your right foot while you drop your right hand back in preparation to throw a ridge hand.

34. As your foot lands back on the ground, twist your shoulders to the right and swing your arm toward his head.

35. Hit him in the head with a right ridge hand. Remember to rotate your right shoulder into the blow.

Crescent Kick / Palm Strike

36. A hoodlum is threatening you.

37. Kick in a "crescent" around his front knee into his groin.

38. Follow up with a left palm strike to his face. The key to generating power is to swing your left shoulder forward as you hit. It's a bit like the motion of throwing a ball.

39. Follow all the way through with the palm strike.

Vertical Elbow

40. You are being harassed by a thug.

41. Suddenly he reaches for you with his right hand.

42. Place your right hand behind his neck and bend your left arm in preparation to strike. You can try to lower his defenses with a seductive statement as you put your hand on his neck.

43. Pull his head forward and drive your elbow under his chin.

Defense Against a Punch to the Stomach

44. A stranger blocks your path and won't let you pass.

45. He grabs you and cocks his right hand to punch you in the stomach.

46. Drop your arms in a x-block across his incoming fist. Bending your knees will help you maintain balance on impact.

 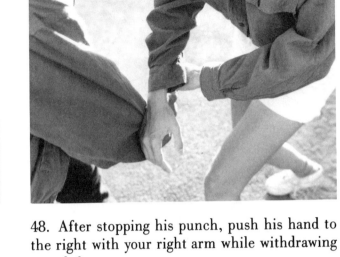

47. Here's a close-up look at the x-block from the left side.

48. After stopping his punch, push his hand to the right with your right arm while withdrawing your left arm.

49. Drop your left shoulder and elbow back as you prepare to elbow him in the face.

50. Start to rotate your shoulders to the right, swinging your elbow as you go.

51. Hit him in the head with a horizontal elbow strike.

7
WHEN SOMEONE GRABS YOU

When an unarmed mugger assaults you his hands and feet are his primary weapons. The moment he grabs hold of you, however, he is surrendering that hand or arm as a weapon for as long as he holds onto you. He can't punch you in the face with a hand that's being used to hold your wrist or some other part of your body. On the other hand, a man stealing a few feet away from you with his hands hidden behind his back or in his coat pocket may be holding a knife or gun.

People tend to think of being grabbed as something scary because the mugger has hold of you, but another way of looking at it is you also have hold of him! Imagine being held by the wrist: If you step back suddenly your opponent will be pulled toward you. You can even attack him by simultaneously throwing a straight punch at his head as you pull him in. If an opponent grabs you by the arm all it really means is that the two of you are connected. It doesn't necessarily mean that your opponent has the advantage. Depending on how you respond, holding on to you may turn out to be a definite disadvantage for a would-be mugger.

Another advantage to being grabbed (although it takes a little practice) is that you can read your opponent's intentions through "feel" based on what his body does. Wing Chun Kung-Fu uses a series of exercises known as "Chi-Sao," or "Sticking Hands," to help develop this skill and if you're interested I would recommend you seek out some instruction on these sensitivity drills. If you were being held by the wrist, for example, and suddenly felt the attacker's arm move to the outside, chances are he is planning to hit you in the head. The sensitivity drills train your body to feel this happening quicker than you can think about it. You simply react and block the strike without any thought process.

One way you can try to develop this skill without enrolling in a Wing Chun class is to practice with your eyes closed. When doing this you should move slowly so you don't hurt your partner. The idea is to try to feel what your opponent's body is doing based on the physical input you are receiving from his hands and other body parts. Wing Chun Kung-Fu, by the way, was invented by a woman...translated it means "Beautiful Spring Time."

Your advantage quickly diminishes if your attacker manages to get you in a choke hold or an armlock. The above statements really only apply when you've simply been grabbed, not put in a choke or some other type of hold in which your movement is severely restricted. To avoid being put in these types of holds you need to respond in the early stages of the attack before your assailant gets a chance to complete his hold on you. For instance, a mugger might bend your arm behind your back a moment before he additionally puts a choke hold on you with his other arm. Through practice you can train yourself to react the second a stranger lays his hands on you.

Front Bear Hug

1. You are picked up in a "bear hug" with your arms pinned to your sides. (*Photo by Marva Hurst.*).

2. Biting your assailant's ear is one way to make him let go. (*Photo by Marva Hurst.*)

3. If he tries to kiss you, biting his lip is also a good defense. (*Photo by Marva Hurst.*)

4. After biting your assailant, pull your head back and prepare to throw a head-butt. (*Photo by Marva Hurst.*)

Rear Bear Hug

5. Smash your forehead into his nose. (*Photo by Marva Hurst.*)

6. You are grabbed from behind and lifted off the ground in a "bear hug" with your hands pinned at your sides. (*Photo by Marva Hurst.*)

7. Grab his groin and squeeze as hard as you can. (*Photo by Marva Hurst.*)

8. Another option is a head-butt. Move your head as far forward as you can and prepare to strike. Chances are you will be struggling in his arms; act as if moving your head forward is part of your struggle. Another way to cover up this movement is to do it at the exact moment you grab his groin. (*Photo by Marva Hurst.*)

9. Smash the back of your head into his face. (*Photo by Marva Hurst.*)

Grabbed from Behind # 1

10. A mugger waits for his victim outside a public bathroom. Always be extra aware in places such as this to avoid being taken by surprise.

11. You feel a stranger's hands on you.

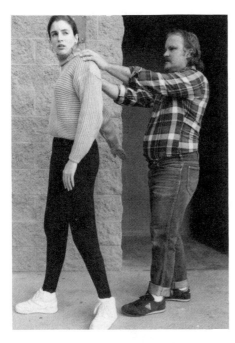

12. and 13. The minute you feel his hands on you, prepare to throw a right ridge hand. If you train in this type of technique, your reaction will become automatic.

14. Spin your body to the left, pivoting your feet as you go, and swing your extended right arm in preparation to land a ridge hand. The key to maximum power is to keep the arm straight and build momentum by letting it follow the body's motion.

15. Strike him in the temple with a ridge hand. This blow is extremely powerful if done correctly.

16. A knee to the groin is one possible follow-up move.

Grabbed from Behind # 2

17. A stranger grabs you from behind.

18. Swing your hips to the right and drive your elbow into his solar plexus.

19. Follow up with a side kick to the knee.

Grabbed by the Shoulder # 1

20. A belligerent mugger grabs you by the shoulder and threatens to strike you.

21. Lace your left arm over his extended arm and place your right arm on his wrist. If his arm isn't extended, moving back a bit just before you make your move may help. You want to place the inside of your left forearm over his elbow joint.

22. Apply pressure to his elbow with your left arm. He will have to bend over to avoid having his arm broken. Lean into his arm to help with the leverage. If the situation merits it, you can break his arm by applying further pressure.

23. Finish him off with a left knee to the face. You can keep him in the armlock and knee him in the face repeatedly until he is incapable of further aggressions toward you.

Grabbed by the Shoulder # 2

24. A stranger has grabbed you by the left shoulder and is threatening you.

25. With your right hand pin his hand to your shoulder.

26. Lean back and throw a side kick to his knee. The idea is to pull him into the kick by keeping his hand on your shoulder as you lean back.

Front Headlock

27. You have been grabbed from the front and placed in a headlock.

28. Drop onto your knee closest to your opponent and punch him in the groin.

Rear Armlock

29. A hoodlum has placed you in an armlock.

30. Back kick him in the knee as hard as you can.

31. Immediately stand up and prepare to throw a karate chop to his face or throat.

32. Twist your shoulders toward your opponent and strike him with a karate chop to the throat.

Grabbed from Behind with an Armlock

33. A hoodlum has grabbed you from behind and is bending your right arm behind your back.

34. Twist to your left and try to strike him in the face with a left horizontal elbow strike. He may block it, but if he doesn't, hit him.

 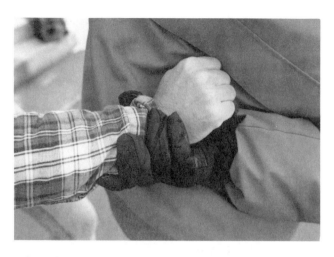

35. and 36. The elbow strike is actually only a distraction to allow you to grab his wrist with your other hand. Do this simultaneously with the elbow strike.

37. As soon as you have reversed his hold on you, turn to your right and twist out of the armlock.

38. Immediately follow up with a side kick to the knee. The idea is to hold onto his arm and pull him into your kick.

Headlock # 1

39. A stranger has placed you in a headlock.

40. Drop your weight by bending your knees to offset his balance. Simultaneously drive the ridge of your hand between his legs into his groin.

Headlock # 2

41. You are being held in a headlock.

42. Move both hands away from your body and prepare to "sandwich" his groin and kidneys between two hammerfists.

43. At the same time strike him in the groin ...and kidneys (not shown).

44. Take advantage of his loosened grip and immediately pull his head backward as you kick his legs forward. You should place your hand in position on his face before you stand up and use the momentum of standing up to help pull him over. With a little practice you'll be able to kick his legs over his head.

Grabbed by One Wrist

45. A hoodlum has grabbed you by the wrist and is trying to pull you in his direction.

46. Kick him in the knee.

47. The kick will probably break his leg and he will fall to the ground.

48. Follow up with a front kick to the face.

Grabbed by the Hair

49. A stranger has grabbed you by the hair.

50. Place your left hand on his hand and step back to fully extend his arm. The idea is to hold onto his hand so he doesn't pull your hair...you also want to keep control of his arm.

51. Swing your right arm and shoulder forward and drive the palm of your right hand under his elbow, breaking it. The idea is to hold his arm in place with your left hand while you strike with the right.

52. Follow up by sweeping his feet out from under him while you shove him backward with your right arm.

Held by Both Wrists # 1

53. A hoodlum has grabbed you and is holding you forcefully by both wrists.

54. Using his hold on you for support, deliver a wing chun kick to his knee.

Held by Both Wrists # 2

55. Another option is to move your hands upwards and then push down to reverse his hold on you.

56. Shown in a close-up, move your hands upward and roll your wrists inward.

57. Continue the motion downward and grab his wrists.

58. Once you have hold of his wrists, throw a front kick into his groin.

8
IN CLOSE QUARTERS

Close quarters refers to areas in which there is limited room for movement, such as in a phone booth or when pinned against a wall. In these situations you can take advantage of the fact that your attacker is so close to you that he will not be able to see you begin your defense. For example, a man who has his face inches from yours will be unaware of what your legs are doing.

Landing your blows in these situations is generally easier than when you have to hit a moving target. Usually your attacker is so close to you that you *can't* miss. His closeness may, however, scare you more than when he is standing a few feet in front of you. In fact, a man who pins you against a wall and leans his face inches away from yours is probably *counting* on you being too scared to retaliate. Only an overconfident fool would leave his groin, face, throat, and knees open to attack by standing so close to someone that they merely had to raise a knee or elbow to inflict damage. Knowing your assailant doesn't expect you to fight back may help you overcome fear. It's also okay to act scared if you are. If a mugger feels he has succeeded in intimidating you, he may lower his defenses—making it easier for you to land the first blow.

Chances are that if you are attacked in close quarters you will be grabbed and pushed against a wall of some sort. It may be strategically wise not to fight back at first. The thinking here is that a man who grabs you and takes you by surprise is operating on high adrenaline and may be prepared for you to try to defend yourself. If you "go with it," however, and allow yourself to be pushed against a wall, a lull may follow the initial attack while your assailant tells you what he wants. Take advantage of the lull and launch your attack during these few seconds of inactivity while his defenses are down. Naturally, there are no absolutes and you may be forced to defend yourself the second you are attacked. The above scenario is only one possible option.

Although demonstrated outdoors, all of the techniques that follow can be used in any situation in which your movement is restricted due to an assailant's nearness or lack of space. An elevator, for example, is one place such an attack may be likely to occur.

Pushed Against a Wall from the Back

1. A stranger pins you up against a wall and threatens you.

2. and 3. Move your right leg behind his and prepare to jerk his leg forward. In actuality, you must lock his leg at the same instant you head-butt him (see next picture).

4. Simultaneously jerk your attacker's leg forward and extend your arms, while smashing the back of your head into his face.

5. Continue to pull his leg forward, keeping him off balance.

6. Twist to the left and smash your elbow into his face while holding onto his leg with your foot.

7. The impact of the blow will most likely drive him to the ground.

8. Stomping on his head ensures he will be incapable of further aggressions.

9. Run away.

Attacked in a Phone Booth # 1

10. Being approached while you are in a phone booth limits your options due to the restrictions of space.

11. Smashing the phone into the intruder's face is one option.

Attacked in a Phone Booth # 2

12. An intruder moves into the phone booth and starts to grope your leg.

13. Drop the phone and instantly throw a right punch into his face.

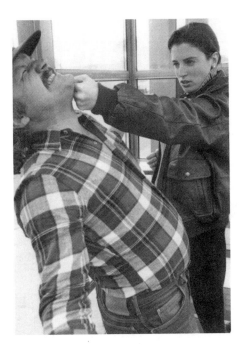

14. Immediately follow up with a straight left punch.

Pinned Against a Wall

15. You are pinned against a wall by an adversary who has placed his forearm across your throat.

16. Take advantage of the fact that his hands are high and throw a knee to the groin. Placing your hands against the wall will help support your body. You can also "push off" the wall a bit to help drive your knee forward.

17. Continue your defense with a right elbow strike to the side of the head. Remember to twist your body into the blow.

Back Against a Wall # 1

18. A bothersome stranger has pushed you up against a wall and won't let you pass. He is blocking your path with his arm.

19. A right vertical elbow strike under his chin is one way to resolve the situation.

20. A left horizontal elbow blow to the face is an excellent follow-up strike.

Back Against a Wall # 2

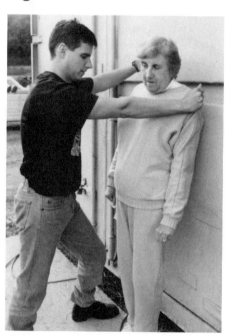

21. A mugger has pinned you against a wall and refuses to let you go.

22. A strike under his chin with the heel of your right palm will stun him and allow you to knock his arm free of your shoulder.

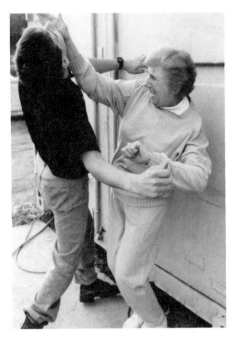

23. The key to success is to extend your arm under his chin, snapping his head back.

Back Against a Wall # 3

24. Take advantage of his stunned state and run away.

25. A stranger has you backed up against a wall and is threatening to hurt you.

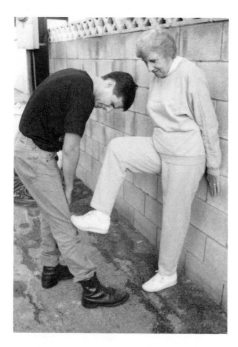

26. Raise your leg and stomp on his kneecap.

27. The key to success is to extend your arm under his chin, snapping his head back.

Back Against a Wall # 4

28. Smash your right elbow onto the back of his neck.

29. A mugger has you backed against a wall and won't let you pass.

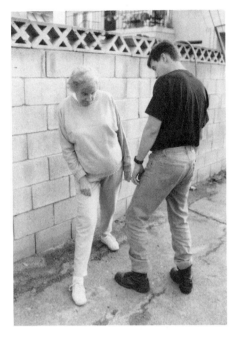

30. and 31. Step off to his side...

...with your right leg.

32. and 33. Kick him in the knee as hard as
you can...

...and then run away.

Back Against a Wall # 5

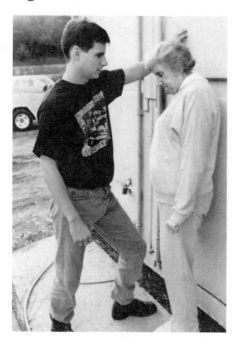

34. A mugger has you backed against a wall and will not let you pass.

35. Smash your knee into his groin.

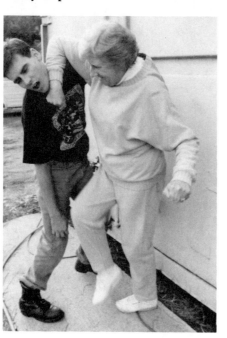

36. Immediately follow up with a right elbow to the side of his face.

Someone Tries to Kiss You

37. A pervert has pinned you against a wall and is attempting to kiss you. (*Photo by Marva Hurst.*)

38. Take advantage of the fact that his face is so close to yours and viciously bite his lip. (*Photo by Marva Hurst.*)

39. Prepare to throw a right elbow. (*Photo by Marva Hurst.*)

40. Swing your shoulder to the left, smashing your elbow into his face. (*Photo by Marva Hurst.*)

Elbow Sandwich

41. You are pinned up against a wall by a stranger.

42. Simultaneously bring your left elbow and right hand up and prepare to sandwich his head between them.

43. Your right hand should strike his head at the same moment as your left elbow.

44. "Sandwich" his head as hard as you can.

9
SITTING DOWN

Defending yourself from a sitting position is easier than you might imagine. Your attacker is basically limited to three angles of attack: he can approach you from the front, rear, or side. Also, the number of targets you have exposed are more limited when you are in a sitting position. For instance: your kidneys, spine, and the back of your legs are well protected.

What follows are some basic concepts and defenses that can be used when attacked while sitting down. These defense techniques can be applied in a car, on a chair, on a bench, or anywhere you encounter an attack while sitting down!

Grabbed from the Front

If you are approached from the front you should have plenty of time to see an attack coming. Anytime a stranger walks toward you, you should consider the possibility that he may have aggressive intentions!

1. A stranger approaches you.

2. Suddenly, he lunges forward and grabs you from the front.

[123]

3. The simplest response is a straight punch to the groin.

4. Follow the punch with a shoulder strike to his stomach or solar plexus. The idea is to explode out of your sitting position after throwing the groin punch, taking advantage of his momentary incapacitation. Also, by pushing him back you are creating room to escape.

5. After striking your opponent, run away.

Arm Around Your Shoulder

This is a common type of sexual harassment. By defending yourself when you are initially grabbed, you stop his aggressions toward you before the situation worsens.

6. An assailant sits down next to you, puts his arm around your shoulder, and starts making unwanted advances.

7. The elbow is pulled back in preparation for a strike. You can mask your intentions by pulling your elbow back as you struggle to get away from him.

8. An elbow strike to the face stuns the attacker and loosens his grip.

9. Take advantage of the opportunity and run away.

His Hands on Your Legs # 1

10. While sitting in the park, a stranger sits down next to you and starts to grope your legs.

11. Take advantage of the fact that his hands are low and throw a straight punch to his face.

His Hands on Your Legs # 2

12. Once again you are bothered by a stranger who is grabbing your legs.

13. Preparing to throw an elbow strike, turn your upper body away from your attacker.

14. Twist your shoulders and upper body toward your attacker and drive your left elbow into his face.

15. Follow up with a right horizontal elbow strike to his face.

Grabbed from Behind

16. Being grabbed from behind requires a quick reaction. A loud yell the moment you feel a stranger's hands on you may stun him for a moment, giving you time to react before he gets a strong hold on you.

17. Grab the arm that is around your throat and simultaneously throw a backfist into his face.

Grabbed by the Face

A man may grab or try to hold your face before he attempts to give you an unwanted kiss.

18. A bus stop is one area an attack might occur while you are sitting down.

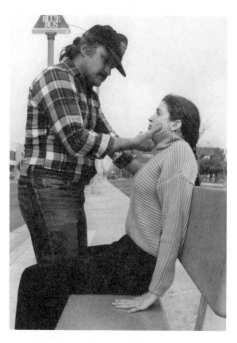

19. Generally, for a mugger to grab you by the face while you are sitting he will have to move very close to you.

20. Take advantage of his nearness and knee him in the groin.

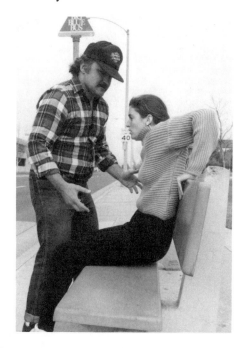

21. In preparation to throw a head-butt, place your hands on the back of the bench.

22. Extend your arms and drive your body up and forward, smashing the top of your head into his face.

23. Immediately stand up and drive your knee into his groin.

24. Follow up with a right elbow strike to the face. Remember to twist your upper body in the direction of the blow (left) to achieve maximum power.

Standing on the Chair

With all self-defense techniques you should think about how you would respond if attacked while in an unusual position.

25. Suppose you were approached while sitting in this position.

26. Rather than jumping to the ground, you may want to take advantage of the height you will have by simply standing up.

27. The knee is raised in preparation for a front kick.

28. Throw a front kick into his face or under his chin.

A Stranger Tries to Touch You

29. Since he has left his groin area open, a man approaching you in this manner is probably confident that you will not retaliate.

30. A straight punch to the groin is the quickest defense.

31. Immediately stand up to prepare to throw a side kick.

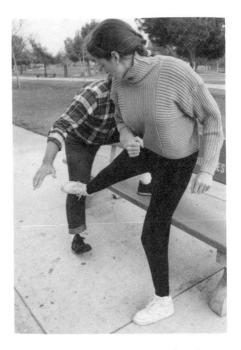

32. Deliver a side kick to his knee.

Bothered by a Man Sitting Next to You

33. An elbow strike to the stomach is an excellent way to stop an annoying stranger from bothering you.

34. If further defense is needed, immediately stand up and twist to the right to prepare to throw a back-handed karate chop.

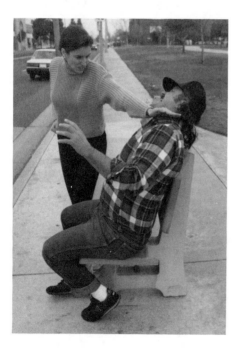

35. and 36. Untwist your body to the left and deliver a back-handed karate chop. Remember that power comes from turning your upper body into the blow.

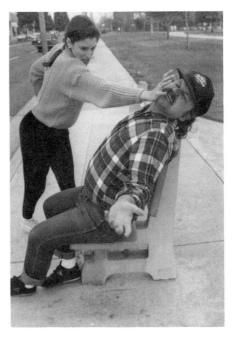

37. and 38. Swing your hips and shoulders to the left...

...and drive a right-handed heel of palm strike into his face.

In a Car

39. What would you do if a stranger suddenly jumped into your car?

Ideally, if you keep your car doors locked with the windows rolled up you should never be in a situation in which you have an unwanted stranger in the passenger seat next to you. If you ever do find yourself in this situation, remembering the words of a paramedic friend of mine may be useful. He recently told me, "I've never pulled out of a car a dead body that was wearing a seat belt." The obvious moral of the story is that you should always wear your seat belt—especially since it is unlikely that an unwanted passenger who has jumped into your car will remember to buckle up.

40. If you are being held hostage in your own car and are wearing your seat belt, one option is to drive head-on into the nearest tree or wall. The intruder will most likely go head first through the windshield.

Another option is to suddenly hit the brakes and hit him at the same instant.

41. Keep both hands on the steering wheel and prepare to hit the brakes suddenly; you must, of course, be wearing your seat belt.

42. Slam on the brakes and at the same instant hit him in the throat with a back-handed karate chop. You should be prepared to get out of the car immediately after striking him. If it's possible, you may want to wait to make your move until you are driving near some people who can come to your assistance when you flee from the car.

Obviously the above suggestions cannot be (and shouldn't be) practiced in a moving car. You can go through the motions while parked but do not practice while the vehicle is in motion.

10
AGAINST A WEAPON

Disarming a man who has a knife, club, or some other type of weapon requires advanced skill. Unfortunately, however, if you are attacked and your opponent has a weapon you're going to have to respond. Keep in mind that the following techniques are difficult to use effectively and should only be attempted in a "life or death" situation in which you have no other choice but to defend yourself.

Against a Club # 1

For demonstration purposes, the following techniques are shown with the attacker holding a large flashlight. Keep in mind that these techniques can also be used against any other "club-like" weapon you may encounter.

1. A thug is threatening to strike you with a club.

2. As he swings the weapon toward your head, block it with a x-block.

3. A closeup of the x-block.

4. From the x-block position, grab his arm with your right hand and guide it to the right as you step off to the left.

5. Knee him in the stomach.

6. You can strike repeatedly with your knee until he is incapacitated.

Against a Club # 2

7. A stranger threatens to club you with his weapon.

8. He moves toward you with his weapon hand held high in preparation to hit you in the head.

9. Step and lean to the "outside" of his body. Outside refers to the back side of his weapon hand. His weapon hand should be between your head and his. If you were to step to the "inside" you would be in between his arms where he could inflict greater damage.

10. Knee him in the groin.

11. Note how by stepping and leaning to the "outside" of his body you get out of his line of attack. This is important since it helps prevent you from taking a direct hit.

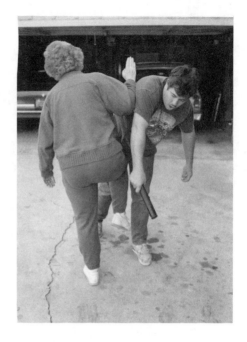

DEFENDING YOURSELF AGAINST A KNIFE

Defending yourself against a man with a knife is dangerous and difficult at best. If you can avoid a physical encounter with a knife-wielding opponent by giving him what he wants, do it. He may only be using the knife for intimidation purposes and not really be prepared to stab you. Don't force his hand unnecessarily.

If, however, you feel you are confronted with a situation in which your life is in danger and your attacker is going to try to hurt or kill you, then you must take action to defend yourself. Almost all of the techniques pictured here begin with your opponent making the first move in the form of a stab or slash at you. Obviously if you are being attacked in such a manner the choice has been made. Your opponent is trying to kill you and you must respond.

As is true with all the techniques pictured in this book, you cannot predict how your opponent will respond or move when he attacks you. These techniques are presented to give you an idea of what some of the possibilities are. To get a better feel for situations that involve being attacked with a knife you need to let your practice partner attack you in any way he desires. Of course you should first try to master the techniques pictured in this

book to give yourself the basic physical skills needed to defend yourself.

All practicing should be conducted with a rubber knife. You don't want to get accidentally stabbed or cut!

Against a Knife # 1

12. A mugger prepares to slash across the left side of your body with his knife.

13. As he swings the knife at you, move forward and block his arm with a left side x-block. Contact is made with the forearm of your left arm and the ridge of your right hand. The key is to rotate your upper body toward his arm as you block.

14. Here's a view of the x-block from the back.

15. Extend your left arm down under his arm and then roll it upward, forcing his arm to rise toward your shoulder. Keep your right hand on his upper arm to help keep his arm straight. Your left arm should almost immediately roll around his arm and toward his elbow. Applying pressure to his elbow also keeps his arm straight.

16. Apply downward pressure to his elbow with your left arm and bend him forward.

17. Force his arm forward by lacing your fingers together and applying pressure. Break his arm by applying full pressure against his elbow.

Against a Knife # 2

18. A thug prepares to stab you with a knife he is holding in his right hand.

19. As he stabs, arch your stomach out of range and grab his wrist. Be prepared to "hop" backward if his lunge has more forward force than you anticipated.

20. Here's a close-up look at the wrist grab.

21. Rotate your body to the left and move his arm away from your center.

22. and 23. Continue to rotate in a left circle...

...and raise his knife hand over your head.

24. Continue to turn and drive the blade into his stomach. This sequence of moves must be done in one "flowing" action to be effective.

Against a Knife # 3

25. A man prepares to slash you with a knife he is holding in his left hand.

26. He slashes at you.

27. Step forward with your left foot and execute a downward "chop" across his wrist with your right hand, stopping his attack. You also may have to step to your left side to help absorb the impact.

28. At the same instant throw a left front punch at his face.

Against a Knife # 4

Sometimes you may have to initiate the attack to prevent yourself from being stabbed.

29. Waiting for this guy to begin his attack could cost you your life.

30. This is a "last ditch" defense. Raise your right hand above your head and yell in an attempt to redirect his attention upward. At the same instant grab the knife with your left hand. Yes, you may get cut, but it's better to take a cut on your hand while you push the knife to the side than to do nothing and risk being stabbed in the stomach. Keep in mind that his knife may only be sharp along the underside of the blade. The "backside" or top of the knife may be dull. You can minimize your risk by not firmly grabbing the belly of the blade as you grab.

31. A closeup of grabbing the blade.

32. Instantly follow up with a front kick to the groin.

33. Maintain control of his knife hand while you attack.

34. Prepare to follow up with a right elbow.

35. Drive your elbow into his face.

Against a Knife # 5

36. A robber is holding you at knife point and is demanding your money. Hold your purse in front of you while you "look" for your money.

37. Without warning, ram your purse into his knife.

38. The idea is to trap the blade by getting it stuck in the purse.

39. Move your purse with the knife stuck in it to the right.

40. Grab his left shoulder with your left arm and knee him in the groin. Maintain control of your purse (and his knife) with your right hand.

Against a Knife # 6

41. You are being held up by a robber who is demanding your money.

42. Start to look in your purse for your money. Talk to him while you're doing this to keep his defenses down.

43. Suddenly throw your purse directly at his face while you let out a loud scream.

44. As the purse reaches his face and limits his field of vision, kick him in the groin.

45. At this point you can run away or prepare to hit him again.

46. Knee him in the head.

Against a Knife # 7

47. You are being threatened by a knife-wielding thug.

48. Swing your purse at him while you yell.

49. Strike his body with your purse. While it is unlikely you will do any serious harm with this blow you may startle him and cause his hands to rise upwards.

50. Side kick him in the knee and break his leg.

11
USING WEAPONS

Learning self-defense techniques that require the use of weapons serves a couple of functions. One of the most important reasons to "sample" them is to familiarize yourself with the way you might be attacked by someone using a weapon.

Relying solely on a weapon as your main means of self-defense is usually a mistake since you may be unarmed when you are actually attacked. While a heavy flashlight is an excellent self-defense weapon, it is unlikely you will want to carry one with you everywhere you go!

The following information is presented only as a sample of what's possible. If after trying a few of the umbrella techniques, for example, you find you feel comfortable with that type of weapon, then you may want to enroll in a stick fighting class.

As with all self-defense techniques, utmost care should be exercised when practicing. Obviously you don't want to "club" your training partner accidentally. One solution is to buy rubber weapons to practice with. Martial arts stores sell a wide variety of rubber knives, clubs, etc. Martial arts magazines also sell a lot of mail order rubber weapons for training purposes.

FLASHLIGHT

A long, heavy "multi-cell" flashlight makes an excellent weapon. The fact that they're not illegal to own and are also useful tools to have around the house or in your car makes them additionally appealing.

Although the following techniques are shown with a flashlight, they could also be executed with any "club-like" weapon such as a heavy stick or pipe.

Flashlight # 1

1. A stranger approaches and threatens to harm you. Do not let him know you are "armed."

2. By holding the flashlight slightly behind you it can be concealed from your attacker until you bring it into action.

3. When he is within striking range, drive the butt of the flashlight into his face.

4. If he raises his hands toward your face before you hit him, you may want to aim low.

5. Drive the butt of the flashlight into his stomach.

Flashlight # 2

6. A stranger approaches and threatens you. Hold the flashlight in front of your chest and stand with your right side forward.

7. Step backward with your front leg and cross it in front of your rear leg.

8. Spin to your left and swing the flashlight in your left arm as you turn. Keep the arm straight and let the weight of the flashlight help you build up speed.

9. Continue to turn and prepare to strike your opponent in the head.

10. Hit him in the head.

Flashlight # 3

11. A mugger moves toward you and tries to punch at your head. Stand facing him, holding the flashlight in front of you in both hands.

12. As he throws his punch, swing the flashlight straight up under his arm.

13. Make contact under his elbow.

14. Follow through with your upward swing, shattering his elbow and driving his arm upward.

15. Let go of the flashlight with your left hand and prepare to hit him in the head.

16. With your right hand smash the flashlight into his head.

Flashlight # 4

17. An antagonist moves toward you.

18. As he reaches out to grab you, prepare to swing the flashlight into his arm with your right hand.

19. Swing the flashlight into his arm.

20. Follow through with your swing across the left side of your body. If you have swung the flashlight with the proper force the follow-through will be natural.

21. Swing the flashlight to the right and hit him in the head.

Flashlight # 5

22. A mugger reaches out to grab your arm. Step back with your left foot and hold the flashlight in your left hand. Naturally you will not be able to predict which hand a mugger will reach out with. What you can do, however, is always step back with the foot that's holding the flashlight. If the mugger were to reach out with his other hand, you could hit him in the head instead of his elbow.

23. As he reaches for you, grab his arm with your "free" hand and prepare to strike him. If he had reached out with his other arm, you could simply prepare to strike him without grabbing his arm.

24. Swing the flashlight into his elbow — if you hit with enough force you will break his arm.

25. Maintain your grip on his arm and deliver a front kick to his groin or chest.

Flashlight # 6

26. A mugger approaches and threatens to beat you up. Assume a left side forward fighting stance and hold the flashlight in front of you.

27. As he moves within range prepare to throw a front kick. You want him to block this kick; preparing to throw the kick a little slower than normal or raising your knee a moment early will help ensure he has time to react.

28. Throw a front kick at his groin. The idea is to make him lower his hands to block the kick so you can hit him in the head with the flashlight. Keep in mind that he may not block your front kick. If this turns out to be the case, by all means kick him!

29. Take advantage of the fact his hands are low and prepare to strike him in the head.

30. Swing the flashlight with your left arm.

31. Hit him in the head.

Flashlight # 7

32. A robber demands you give him your money. Assume a left side forward fighting stance and hold the flashlight in front of you.

33. As he moves toward you, bend your legs and prepare to hit him in the knees.

34. Swing the flashlight into his knees.

35. Follow through with the swing to your left.

36. Reverse the direction and swing the flashlight into his head.

37. Follow through with your swing.

KNIFE

Learning how to use a knife effectively as a self-defense tool takes a lot of time and instruction. One of the biggest dangers is that an attacker may take the knife away from you and stab *you* with it. Chances are he may have practiced such tactics for just such an occasion.

If you want to carry a knife for self-defense I recommend you first acquire some quality instruction in one of the Philippine martial arts, many of which train extensively in the use of knives. The information that follows is only presented to give you a conceptual idea of what is possible. Also — as previously stated — by practicing using a knife you'll start to get an idea of how you may be attacked if you are ever confronted by an assailant wielding a blade.

Another consideration with using a knife is the legality of the weapon. *Be sure to check your local laws before carrying a weapon of any type.*

Knife # 1

38. An advantage to some knives is that they can be concealed in a pocket. This approaching mugger has no idea this woman is armed.

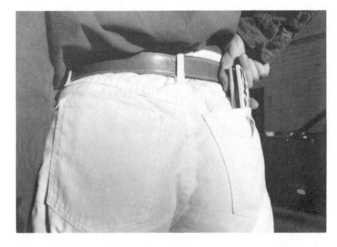

39. As soon as you sense the possibility of danger take the knife out of your pocket. The idea is not to alert your assailant to the fact that you are armed.

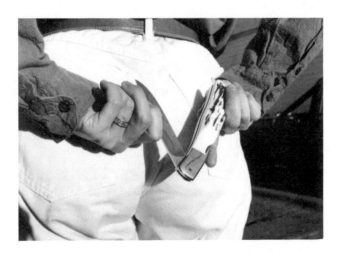

40. Unfold the knife behind your back.

41. As your opponent approaches, hold the weapon out of view. "Locking knives" such as this one are nice because the danger of the knife closing in your hand is eliminated since the blade "locks" into place.

42. and 43. Holding the knife in this manner hides it from your assailant...

...yet you are ready for action.

44. Hold the knife in your right hand.

45. and 46. As your opponent reaches for you . . .

. . . swing your right hand and punch toward his face with a "hooking" motion.

Knife # 2

47. Instead of punching him, let the knife slice across his face.

48. You are being held against a wall by an assailant who is unaware of the fact that you are armed (see photos # 39 and # 40).

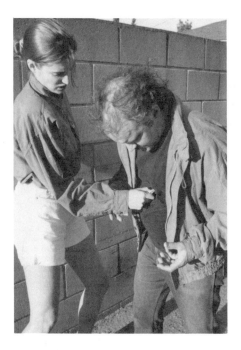

49. The mugger prepares to punch you in the face.

50. Stab him in the stomach.

Knife # 3

51. You are being threatened by a stranger. Hold the knife as shown in photo # 42.

52. As your opponent reaches for you, start to bring your left hand up under his elbow while you simultaneously raise the knife and prepare to slash across his wrist.

53. At the same time bring the knife down across his wrist in a slashing motion and slam his elbow upward with your left hand. The idea is to "lock" his arm at the moment of impact.

54. Follow through with the downward slash across his wrist.

55. Continue withdrawing your hand down and back. Prepare to drive the blade into his armpit.

56. Swing your right arm upward and forward, stabbing him in the armpit or arm.

UMBRELLA

The following techniques are shown with an umbrella, but any stick-type weapon — a cane, for example — could also be used. One of the major advantages to these types of weapons is that they have reach. If you are close enough to a mugger to hit him with your fists, he can also do the same to you. Using an umbrella or a cane means you can defend yourself from a distance...lowering your chances of being hit.

Umbrella # 1

57. You are approached by a robber who demands you give him your money. Hold the umbrella in your right hand.

58. As he reaches for you, swing the umbrella into his ribs under his arm. If he reaches for you with his other arm, stab him with the umbrella rather than swinging it.

Umbrella # 2

59. Immediately follow up with a front kick to his knee.

60. A hoodlum approaches behind you; prepare yourself for action.

61. He grabs you from behind and starts to turn you around. You are holding the umbrella in your right hand.

62. Spin to your left faster than he is turning you and bring the umbrella up and prepare to stab him.

63. Stab him in the stomach.

Umbrella # 3

64. A man is standing in front of you and won't let you pass.

65. Raise your arm up in the air and yell. The idea is to make him look up. With his attention directed upward he will be less likely to block your attack.

66. Take advantage of the moment and stab him in the stomach.

Umbrella # 4

67. A hoodlum threatens to harm you. Assume a right side forward stance and hold the umbrella in your right (forward) hand.

68. Raise the umbrella in an arch toward his neck; it should travel in a half circle from the ground to his neck.

69. and 70. Drive the point of the umbrella . . .

(70.) ...into his neck.

Umbrella # 5

71. A mugger is blocking your path and won't let you pass.

72. Suddenly he reaches out to grab you. As he does, step back and prepare to stab him.

73. Lunge forward and stab him with the umbrella.

12
GUNS

In the hands of a trained individual, a gun is the best self-defense tool in the world. Imagine waking up at three in the morning to the sounds of your front door being kicked in...Wouldn't you rather face your assailant with a gun in your hand than to have to engage him in unarmed hand-to-hand combat? A gun enables you to defend yourself at a safe distance from your attacker. If you were awakened in the middle of the night by unknown intruders, your reaction time, coordination, and thought process would most likely be slower than normal. A gun allows you to take cover and defend yourself without exposing yourself to additional risk.

To understand the effectiveness of a gun as a self-defense tool, imagine yourself as a mugger.

WHAT ARE THE DISADVANTAGES?

If you have children, obviously your gun cannot be kept in a place where they may find it. This also goes for curious roommates or houseguests. You don't want to leave a loaded gun anywhere it could be found accidentally. The potential disadvantage is that this may force you to keep the gun in an impractical place in the event you suddenly need it for an immediate self-defense situation. A woman who lives alone can keep a gun under her bed where it can be brought into play instantly. A woman with four children, for example, obviously couldn't.

Some solutions are gun safes, keeping your gun unloaded, or setting up alarm systems that give you enough advance warning to allow you to get your gun.

Gun safes range in size from large vaults to small boxes that only hold one handgun. The small safes can be bolted to the floor in a discreet location near your bed, making the gun quickly accessible in an emergency if you need it. I rec-

What would frighten you more: the thought of encountering a victim who tries to defend herself without a weapon...or the thought of encountering a woman who pulls out a large gun and shoots you?

Naturally, there are times when the use of a gun is impractical or illegal. A *carry permit* is necessary to carry a gun on your person. Depending on where you live, a permit may be easily obtained or virtually impossible to get. This is one of the many reasons why it's important to also learn how to defend yourself "empty-handed." Also, not all self-defense situations justify the use of lethal force. If you're being harassed in a bar by a drunk who simply wants to dance, you can't shoot him for being obnoxious!

ommend a small handgun safe with a lock that requires a key to be opened. The best method is to insert the key in the lock when you go to bed and to remove the key when you're not home. This way if you wake up in the middle of the night and need your gun, all you have to do is turn the key and remove the weapon.

Some safes have push button locks, but these should be avoided. In theory, a child might discover the safe and spend hours playing and pushing the buttons, possibly hitting the combination by accident! Another option is a trigger lock. This is a device that clamps over the gun's trigger, making it impossible to fire. A key is needed to remove the lock and you can carry this with you when you leave home.

Keeping your gun *unloaded* is a less desirable option since you will have to load your gun while under the stress of knowing an attacker is approaching.

Alarm systems are an excellent idea regardless

of whether you live alone or not. If you're not awake when an intruder enters your bedroom, you won't be able to defend yourself. An alarm will give you enough warning to get your gun. An advance warning system such as an alarm becomes more important if you have to keep your gun in an inconvenient location for security reasons.

Rather than list all the possible options available in alarm systems, I recommend you contact a reputable home alarm salesman about possibilities available. Basically it should create a lot of noise as soon as someone attempts an entry into your home. In addition, the alarm should also be connected to local law enforcement offices so that they are alerted a break-in is in process and you need assistance. Some alarm companies have their own monitoring stations for this purpose.

A dog can also function as an alarm and give you some advance warning if an intruder is in your home. Another advantage to owning a dog

TYPES OF GUNS

For civilian self-defense purposes, there are three types of guns that can be considered: shotguns, semi-automatics, and revolvers.

Shotguns

Shotguns have the advantage of having the most stopping power of any gun available. Stopping power refers to the gun's ability to stop an opponent when you shoot him. If you shoot someone with a small caliber bullet such as a .22, he may not die for ten minutes. This delay gives the attacker time to retaliate. Imagine having an intruder enter your bedroom with a gun in his hand. When you shoot him it's important he cannot shoot back after he's been hit. A shotgun practically ensures this.

Shotguns shoot a wad of small metal balls that spread out in a circular pattern as they travel through the air. The metal ball loads (referred to as "shot loads") come in a variety of sizes: "00" is the largest. If you shoot somebody from ten feet away with the "00," you will make a six-inch wide hole in their body — they won't shoot back.

is that you can send the dog out to investigate strange noises. I'm sure you've thought you heard something in the middle of the night before, but you weren't sure if it merited calling the police. Sending your dog to investigate is safer than going to look yourself!

Another disadvantage to a gun is that it requires *specialized training* to use it competently. If you go out and buy a gun but don't receive any training, go home and load it and leave it under your bed for two years, and then suddenly need to defend yourself with it, your attacker may take your weapon from you and shoot you with it! If you buy a gun, take the time to get competent instruction on its use — and then practice! To defend yourself competently with a firearm, you must first get past the fear of guns that most untrained people have. This won't happen in just one or two practice sessions. I recommend you go to a shooting range a minimum of once a month.

The disadvantage to shotguns is the amount of "kick" encountered when shooting them. To use a shotgun effectively, it must be shot with the butt of the gun against your shoulder (like a rifle). Learning how to handle the gun's recoil and getting over the fear of it requires considerable training.

Another disadvantage is the gun's length. The legal minimum length requirement for a shotgun is eighteen inches in California (this varies from state to state). It's not uncommon for intruders to pose as deliverymen, repairmen, etc., to get you to open your door and gain entrance into your home. Suppose you want to answer your door with the security of a gun in your hand but don't want to frighten an innocent deliveryman. A handgun can be held discreetly behind the back. Opening your door while trying to conceal a shotgun is virtually impossible... and won't do much for your image around the neighborhood.

If you do decide to get a shotgun, I recommend you buy a 12 gauge. It's what the police use and is the best choice for self-defense.

Semi-Automatics

Semi-automatic handguns differ from revolvers in a number of ways. These guns are called automatics because they "automatically" feed a fresh bullet into the firing chamber after every shot while spitting out the spent shell from the previous shot. Also, they usually have a "clip" in the handle that holds the bullets. The clip (also referred to as the magazine) makes unloading and loading the gun extremely fast.

The three advantages to these types of guns are the speed at which they can be fired, the ease of reloading them, and the number of bullets they hold. For example, some of these guns are capable of holding sixteen bullets when fully loaded. They can also be fired faster than revolvers because the hammer is automatically cocked after every shot.

The disadvantage to semi-automatics is that they are a lot more complicated to use than a revolver. Loading the clips, cycling the slide, and learning how to work the various safeties and "decocking" levers require more involved training to become competent with the gun. If you're willing to take the time to learn how to work a semi-automatic, however, they are excellent self-defense weapons.

Revolvers

Revolvers are, in my opinion, the best type of gun for civilian self-defense. Loading a revolver is simple, they don't "jam" the way semi-automatics can, and the training required to use one competently is less than that required of other guns. They also don't require as much maintenance. If a revolver is left unattended under your bed for a period of time and you suddenly have to pick it up and pull the trigger, it's going to go "Bang." A semi-automatic, however, might jam — which could cost you your life.

WHAT CALIBER?

Caliber refers to the size of the bullet your gun fires. The more common handgun cartridges are discussed below.

The .22 comes in a variety of lengths, which are referred to as short, long, and long rifle. All of these are impractical for home defense. The .22 caliber round doesn't have enough stopping power to ensure that an assailant won't be able to harm you once he's been shot.

Some people argue that the .22 is a good choice for women because it has virtually no recoil when fired. The thinking is that you'll be able to hit your target with a higher degree of accuracy than with a gun that has more recoil.

Actually, many of the larger calibers are virtually recoil-free when shot through heavy framed guns because the weight absorbs recoil. By the way, it's a myth that only men can control large caliber handguns. A woman can shoot and control any handgun made.

The .32 caliber cartridge is also inadequate as a self-defense round. Like the .22, it lacks stopping power.

The .38 Special is the best choice of defense round available. It has enough stopping power to stop a man dead in his tracks, but isn't so powerful as to make controlling its recoil difficult. The use of a soft, hollow-point bullet is recommended. Hollow-points make the bullet expand as it passes through flesh, which, simply put, creates a bigger hole. Using a soft lead bullet helps ensure that the bullet stays in the victim. The idea is not to have the bullet pass through the body and hit an innocent bystander. This is one of the main problems with some of the large calibers available.

The .357 Magnum is too powerful to be used as a civilian self-defense round. The two main problems are the fact that the bullet will most likely exit the body — and possibly even pass through your apartment wall and hit an innocent neighbor — and the fact that controlling the recoil of the .357 requires considerable training and practice.

However, most .357 Magnum revolvers are also capable of firing the .38 Special caliber bullet. The only difference between a .38 Special and a .357 Magnum is the length of the cartridge. The bullet sizes are identical. The reason is that the .357 Magnum uses more powder. You may want to buy the heavier framed .357 Magnum and then shoot .38 Special ammunition through it. This way you'll have the option of using the more powerful .357 Magnum round at the shooting range for fun! Also, if you practice with a .357 Magnum and then switch to the less powerful .38 Special, controlling the .38 Special should be easy!

The 9mm cartridge is used in semi-automatic pistols and not in revolvers. One of the reasons this round has become so popular is the fact that many of the new guns on the market that use this cartridge are capable of holding sixteen rounds or more. If you were a narcotics agent, who might have to face multiple assailants during a drug raid, this massive fire power could be justified. Civilian defense purposes, however, rarely require more than two or three rounds. If you're willing to take the time to learn how to operate some of the high capacity 9mm pistols on the market, they are excellent and reliable weapons.

The .45 Automatic is an excellent self-defense round. However, it is designed to be used in semi-automatic pistols, which are more complicated to use than revolvers. The .45 also has quite a bit of "kick" and getting used to its recoil can take some time.

The .44 Magnum is a hunting cartridge and realistically shouldn't be considered for civilian self-defense.

WHAT GUN SHOULD YOU BUY?

I recommend you get a heavy framed .357 Magnum revolver with a six-inch barrel and fire .38 Special ammunition through it. The weight of the large .357 Magnum will help absorb recoil, which will be almost nonexistent when you fire .38 Special ammunition through it. The six-inch barrel also gives the gun added weight and increases its "pointability." Also, a six-inch barrel is more accurate than a two- or four-inch barrel.

A large gun also has a deterrent factor. If you point a small caliber handgun with a two-inch barrel at an assailant, you may not frighten him if he knows anything about guns. An intruder who unexpectedly finds himself staring down the business end of a large .357 Magnum will probably think twice about continuing his assault.

If you're planning to "carry" your gun on your person or in a purse, then you may want to get a smaller framed, shorter barreled .38 Special. Most guns, however, are kept in the home and the above advice is based on that fact.

TACTICS

Let's suppose you are awakened to the sound of intruders in your house. The first thing you should immediately do is turn on the lights, get your gun, and if you really believe there is a potential threat, call the police.

Sometimes simply getting up, turning on the lights, and making some noise will be enough to scare an intruder away. He may, for example, have thought the house was uninhabited.

The police may stop taking your calls for help seriously if you have them coming out to your house every two weeks for false alarms. Once you're awake, take a second to assess the situation. If it's a windy night, for example, the sounds you heard may just be a tree branch banging on the side of the house. If, however, you feel you have an intruder in your house, you should immediately call the police.

Don't go hunting for the intruder! You're much safer taking cover in your bedroom with the lights on and your gun aimed toward the door while you call the police. If you go walking around your house in the dark you may possibly get "surprised" by the intruder. Imagine if you were to break into someone's house. Your senses would probably be on full alert and your adrenaline would be pumping full blast. This is the state of awareness the intruder is most likely in. You, the victim, have just woken up, are probably scared, and your reflexes and senses are not yet up to full capacity.

Searching your house for an intruder is a dangerous practice and shouldn't be done! However, I realize that a time may come when you will want to look around your house after hearing a sound that is "probably nothing." Let's say you hear a thud downstairs...but you also know your cat is downstairs. If you do search your house with a gun in your hand, do not hold it out in front of you at arm's length. An intruder waiting behind a door may disarm you before you see him. Hold your gun at waist level, which minimizes the chances of you being disarmed.

Rather than walk around with a flashlight (which an intruder will probably shoot at when he's startled by your light), turn on your houselights. If they don't go on, don't go searching ...call the police. Once again — searching for an intruder is a mistake. If you really feel someone has broken into your home, call the police and take cover.

BEING HELD AT GUNPOINT

It's impossible to learn how to disarm an assailant who is holding you at gunpoint solely from a book. Being aware of your environment can go a long way toward preventing getting yourself in a situation such as this. Things such as not walking alone at night, keeping your car doors locked, not opening your front door to an unknown person, etc., all decrease your chances of being held at gunpoint. If, however, you are unfortunate enough to find yourself in this predicament, the following information may help.

If you have children or don't live alone, you must have a prearranged plan as to what they will do in the event of an emergency. Obviously, it doesn't make much sense to secure yourself in your bedroom with a handgun at the ready if your children may come running in from the hallway. Your plan of action will depend largely on the floor plan of your house, but here are some helpful hints.

You want to gather everybody in one room; ideally the room should have only one entrance. The idea is that once your family is in the "Safe Room," you can guard the entrance with your gun. The Safe Room should also have a telephone line that is different from the rest of the house so that the intruder cannot lift an extension off the hook to stop you from calling the police. A large, walk-in closet in your (or your children's) bedroom may be ideal for this purpose. A bedroom with only one entrance can also be used as a Safe Room. One option is to have the capability of locking yourself into the Safe Room so that you are now safe from the intruder and can simply wait for the police to arrive.

Once you're in the Safe Room and have called the police, wait for them to come and let you out. When you call the police, they will most likely have you stay on the line until they arrive. You want to know when the police have arrived so you don't mistake them for the intruder, and you don't want to be mistaken by the police as the gun-wielding intruder.

You can jam a revolver by grabbing it by the cylinder — providing the hammer of the gun has not yet been cocked.

Some models of semi-automatic pistols can be jammed by pushing directly on the end of the barrel. The .45 Automatic, made by Colt, is one example of a gun this works on. Obviously, if you tried this on a pistol that wouldn't jam in this manner, you will have made a mistake that will cost you your life. All I can tell you is to get as familiar as you can with different types of guns so you can recognize them on sight.

Get out of the line of fire as you make your grab for the gun. If you miss and/or your assailant pulls the trigger, you don't want to take the bullet dead on. Turning sideways helps to minimize the risk of the bullet hitting a vital organ.

Get as close as you can, or stay as far away as you can. If the gunman is holding you at gunpoint from fifteen feet away (such as in a store), he may not hit you when he shoots. You're better off to maintain the distance between you and him rather than moving closer to attempt to disarm him.

If you're going to attempt to disarm a gunman, you want to be as close to him as possible before you make your move. Don't try anything from five or six feet away. In the time it takes you to reach him, he will most likely have time to react and shoot you.

HOLDING AN ASSAILANT AT GUNPOINT

Suppose you "get the drop" on an intruder in your home and are now holding him at gunpoint until the police arrive. First, if he attempts to run away, let him go. You'll have a hard time explaining why you shot him in the back (especially if he's unarmed).

If he doesn't run, make sure you can see both of his hands. The best method is to have him hold them straight out from his sides or straight over his head. Next, have him lie face down on the floor with his hands straight out from his sides.

Don't get too close or he may attempt to disarm you. If you're not prepared for this onslaught, you may find yourself getting shot with your own gun!

Another option is simply to tell the intruder to get out or you'll shoot him. He'll probably run away and you can give the police his description and let them catch him later. This may be safer than holding a nervous criminal who may attempt to disarm you rather than be arrested when he hears the police sirens approaching.

13
ADVANCED TECHNIQUES

MULTIPLE ATTACKERS

What would you do if you were confronted by more than one assailant simultaneously? Basically you use the exact same techniques you would use on a single opponent. All the techniques used in this book are based upon the principle of ending the confrontation within a few seconds by doing immense physical damage to your attacker (such as breaking his leg). What you need to do when you have more than one assailant is to determine which one of them is the immediate threat and take him out first. You also need to try to land the most damaging blows you can. Don't waste time with a punch to the head if you can throw a knee-shattering kick. If an attacker can't walk, he can't fight.

The other important aspect you need to remember when there are multiple attackers is that once you begin your attack, you cannot stop until you have incapacitated all of the assailants. The element of surprise will definitely be on your side. The last thing two hoodlums expect when harassing a single woman is for her to turn the tables on them by launching a vicious onslaught of kicks and punches. Odds are that when you begin your attack, your opponents will momentarily freeze in disbelief.

However, keep in mind that if after disabling one person you have the opportunity to flee, you should. Let's say you're in a bar and are being harassed by two drunks who have overstepped the boundaries of good behavior and have actually become a threat to your safety. The best course of defense in this situation would be to alert the management of the establishment and let them deal with the troublemakers. But let's say as you begin to leave, the two of them block your exit and threaten you, or catch you in the parking lot. The best solution may be to concentrate your attack on the individual who is blocking your escape route. Once you have disabled him, it may be more prudent to flee than to stick around and fight the second assailant.

Every situation will have different circumstances but generally the theory will stay the same. One, if you can run away, do so. Two, if you must defend yourself, take out the assailant who is posing the most immediate threat. Three, once you have begun your assault, don't stop until you either run away or have incapacitated all aggressors.

Multiple Attackers # 1

1. You have been cornered by two thugs who are threatening you.

[173]

2. Step toward the thug closest to you and throw a left straight punch at his face.

4. Follow the kick with a front knee to his face.

3. Immediately throw a right front kick at the second assailant. Depending on how far away from you he is, you may or may not need to move closer to him first.

Multiple Attackers # 2

5. You are being dragged down the street by two kidnappers!

6. Suddenly step back with your left foot. Your action should take the thugs by surprise; their reaction will probably be to pull you forward.

7. As they pull you forward use the momentum to launch a left round kick.

8. Strike the man on your left with a round kick to his kidney.

9. Immediately turn your attention to the assailant on your right.

10. Deliver a side kick to his ribs or knees. You can use his hold on your wrist to pull yourself into the kick.

11. The force of your kick should knock him clear of you.

12. Turn your attention back to the assailant on your left. Prepare to throw a side kick to his knee.

13. Kick him in the knee.

Multiple Attackers # 3

14. You have been cornered by two attackers, one of whom is armed with a lead pipe.

15. The man holding the pipe is a bigger threat to you, so attack him first. Prepare to throw a front kick.

16. Deliver a front kick to his groin.

17. Immediately follow with a ridge hand to his temple.

18. Turn to your left and raise your left leg in preparation to kick. You're actually preparing to throw a spin kick.

19. Prepare to deliver the kick.

20. Kick your opponent in the groin.

21. After you kick him, continue to stay alert so you can strike again if need be.

Multiple Attackers # 4

22. Two men have pushed you up against a wall and won't let you pass. One of them is resting his hand on or near your right shoulder.

23. Grab his wrist with your left hand and prepare to put him in an armlock.

24. Turn your body to the left as you throw your right arm over his elbow and begin to apply downward pressure.

25. Force him forward by pushing down on his elbow. Secure the armlock and break his arm by applying further pressure to his elbow.

26. Maintain control of your opponent with the armlock while you deliver a front kick to the second man.

27. Assess the situation.

28. Since the second man is still standing, deliver a second front kick to his face.

29. Finish off your opponent with a front knee to his face.

Multiple Attackers # 5

30. One mugger has grabbed you from behind and is choking you with a pipe while his accomplice approaches in front of you.

31. Stop the man in front of you with a front kick. At the same instant grab the pipe that is around your neck. Grabbing the pipe accomplishes two things: one, it prevents you from being choked as you kick and two, it provides support and balance as you kick.

32. After you kick, immediately step back with your left foot and prepare to drive your left elbow into the ribs of the man who is choking you. Keep hold of the pipe with your right hand.

33. Smash your elbow into his ribs.

34. If he doesn't release his grip on the pipe, continue to strike until he does.

35. Prepare to hit the other man in the face with the pipe.

36. Swing the pipe into his head.

37. Prepare to throw a side kick at the man who was previously choking you.

38. Break his leg with a side kick.

Multiple Attackers # 6

39. Two men have pinned you up against a wall and are threatening to harm you.

40. Prepare to throw a side kick at the man on your left.

41. Deliver a side kick to his knee.

42. With the same leg immediately throw a front knee into the gut of the other man. You may be able to deliver the blow without putting your foot down between blows.

43. If need be, deliver a second blow with your knee.

44. Grab your opponent by the shoulders. You could also put him in a headlock.

45. and 46. Smash his head...

...into the wall behind you.

OTHER ADVANCED TECHNIQUES

The following techniques are considered advanced because it's more difficult to use them effectively than the ones pictured elsewhere in this book. A low side kick to the knee is easy to execute and therefore considered "basic," while a jumping side kick is extremely difficult to use effectively and so is considered "advanced." Keep in mind that "basic" used in this context means reliable. The following techniques are presented so you can increase your self-defense knowledge if you so desire.

One Arm Take Down

47. A stranger approaches you.

48. As he reaches out to grab you with his right hand, stop him by pushing his arm at the wrist with your left hand.

49. Step behind his forward leg with your right leg and simultaneously throw your right arm across his shoulder as pictured.

50. Kick his front leg out from under him by "hooking" and "pulling" with your leg. At the same instant twist your shoulders to the right and throw him to the ground. Your foot and shoulders are moving in opposite directions.

51. Let him fall to the ground.

52. At this point you can run away or continue your attack if need be.

53. Prepare to throw a karate chop to the neck.

54. Deliver a karate chop to his neck.

Jumping Kick

This kick is generally impractical to use but is a lot of fun to practice! One reason is that it's hard to have any control of your body's direction once you've jumped into the air; if your opponent moves to the side you'll fly right by him! On the other side of the coin, if you kick someone with the momentum of your body's weight flying through the air behind the blow, it's going to hurt!

55. and 56. Run toward your opponent and jump into the air. Lift the knee of the foot you intend to kick with when you first jump.

The raising up of the knee is what starts your momentum upward. Just before you reach your target, kick out with a side kick.

Hatchet Kick

57. A mugger is standing in front of you with his fists held high and is threatening you. Turn your body sideways so you present less of a target, but do not assume a fighting stance. The idea is to be ready but not alert your attacker that you intend to defend yourself.

58. Keeping your rear leg straight, swing it forward and upward toward his front arm.

59. Kick above his arm and then drive your heel downward into his arm.

60. Pull his arm down with the momentum of the kick; chances are his body will partially follow.

61. Prepare to punch him in the face with your front hand.

62. Deliver a front punch to his face. The concept is to let your arm follow the forward momentum created by the kick.

Spinning Crescent Kick

63. A stranger is threatening you.

64. With your right side forward, reach out with your left hand to distract your opponent. You're actually "winding" your body up for the kick to follow.

65. Quickly spin on your right leg to the left (backward) and start to swing your left leg forward and upward, keeping it straight as it travels.

66. Continue your spin and prepare to kick with your left leg. Remember to keep it straight as it travels toward your opponent.

67. Kick your opponent across the face.

68. As your foot hits the ground, lunge toward your opponent to continue your attack.

69. Throw a right punch to his body or face. The concept is to continue the circular motion of the spin with your shoulders to drive your fist into your opponent.

Headlock and Throw

70. A stranger reaches out to grab you.

71. Knock his hand off you with your left hand and simultaneously grab him behind his opposite shoulder. To make this move effective you need to knock his right hand clear of you before he actually grabs you.

72. Grab him by both shoulders and drive your knee into his chest as you pull him forward.

73. Immediately throw your right arm over his neck and put him in a headlock.

74. Drop your shoulder and twist him backward. If he doesn't fall you can roll into him and drive him to the ground.

75. Continue twisting and throw him to the ground.

76. Evaluate the situation.

77. If he is still a threat, drop yourself onto his chest, landing on your knees.

FIGHTING FROM THE GROUND

It's a good idea to become familiar with some of the concepts involved with fighting from the ground in case you are pushed to the ground by your attacker. Also, it's possible you may fall to the ground during a struggle if you are hit. Unfortunately your attacker may seek to do further harm to you once you have fallen.

Lying Down # 1

78. You have been pushed to the ground by a stranger.

79. As he approaches pull your knees into your chest for protection. You're also preparing to throw a side kick to his knee.

80. When he is close enough, side kick him in the knee.

81. Another option is to hook his leg with your lower leg as you side kick him.

82. Twist him to the left with your legs after you kick. Throwing him over will be easy if you first break his leg with the side kick.

Lying Down # 2

83. You have been attacked by a stranger who has forced you onto your back and is trying to choke you.

84. Raise your "outside" leg and prepare to drive it into his face.

85. Drive your left foot into his face.

Lying Down # 3

86. You have been pushed to the ground by a mugger who is now moving toward you to do more damage.

87. As he steps near you, kick his leg out to the side.

88. At the same instant kick him in the groin with your other leg.

89. You can follow up with a second kick to the head.

14
THE AFTERMATH

What would you do in the moments after you have been forced to defend yourself? For example, you've responded to a break-in in your home and have shot a crook; now what do you do? Or after being assaulted on the street, you defend yourself and seriously injure your attackers. Legally speaking what do you do in the aftermath of an attack can affect your future. Whether you're under any moral obligation to assist an injured individual who moments ago was trying to take your life is questionable. What follows are some thoughts on what you may or may not want to do in the aftermath of an attack.

Call an ambulance. Calling an ambulance immediately after injuring an attacker will look good in a court of law. Morally, it obviously is a humane thing to do. Personally speaking, if I had to defend myself against someone who was trying to injure me, I would find it difficult to seek assistance for him. You may, however, feel differently.

If you are in your home and have shot or disabled an attacker, it becomes much more important that you take steps to help your situation should you end up in court. In this case you should definitely call an ambulance to assist the intruder.

Call the police. After calling an ambulance you should immediately call the police. If you are not in your home, you may have to travel away from the scene to reach a phone. Before you leave the scene, take note of street names, landmarks, etc., so you can direct the police and ambulance where to go. In many cities, dialing 911 connects you to emergency personnel and enables you to contact police and medical personnel in one phone call.

If you are in your home, then it is imperative you call the police if you have an injured assailant in your house.

Call a lawyer. If you have a personal attorney

your next action should be to contact him. Having legal counsel is important and the sooner you obtain it, the better. If you want to be very well prepared for the aftermath of an attack, you could do a little research now and figure out what law firm you will call if a need should arise.

Keep the intruder in sight. This applies more to the aftermath of a home defense situation than anywhere else. If you have shot or injured an intruder in your home, you do not want to let him out of your sight while you make a phone call. He may not be as incapacitated as you believe and may attack you while your back is turned. Imagine returning to the room where you shot the thief only to discover he is gone. He may have left...or he may be hiding in a doorway, waiting to kill you so you cannot identify him to the authorities.

If you do not have a phone in the room where your attacker lies, one option would be to leave your house and flee to the neighbors' to use their phone. Another option would be to make noise to attract attention into your apartment or house.

Obviously, if you're in the street and no phone is within sight you must leave the scene if you wish to contact authorities.

Don't get near him. Just because you have injured, or think you have injured, a potential rapist or thief doesn't mean he is incapable of further aggressions. He may be playing possum; it's possible the crook isn't injured at all and is lying on the ground in hopes that you will move near enough for him to grab you while your defenses are down. Again, this is much more critical if you have an injured crook lying on the floor of your home. In the street you can run away after defending yourself.

Note his description. The police will want you to describe not only how tall your attacker was and what his face looked like, but also what he was wearing, the color of his clothes, what jewelry he may have been wearing, and if he had any unusual tattoos, scars, or other identifiable marks. Naturally, while under the stress of defending yourself you may forget to note these things but if you must leave an intruder in your house while you flee for assistance, the ability to give the police an accurate description is obviously very important.

Don't clean up. As distasteful as it sounds, this is very important if you have been the victim of rape. Your physical condition after a rape will be vital evidence in court. If you are unfortunate enough to find yourself in this situation you should immediately go straight to a hospital or call for assistance.

You also should not clean up your home after defending yourself. Tipped over and broken furniture, forced doors and locks, and windows that have been broken to gain entry are all important pieces of evidence the police will need to examine. If, for example, you clean up the broken glass around a broken window through which the thief entered your home, it may be hard to prove your window was broken that night. Your intruder's defense lawyer may claim the window could have been broken weeks ago. The point is, you don't want to accidentally destroy evidence that may be needed if you have to go to court.

Check other household members. If you have children this will be a high priority for you. You should check everyone in your household to make sure they were not injured by the intruder

prior to your awareness of his presence. If you were unfortunate enough to be surprised by a thief who had already gained access to your bedroom before you shot him, you don't know if he has already visited other areas of the house.

Check yourself for injuries. During the heat of battle you may not have noticed that you have sustained an injury. The fortitude required to overcome an opponent along with the adrenaline rush that accompanies such an encounter may have prevented you from feeling the pain of a knife or other weapon. This can be especially true if the damage is not immediately life-threatening. Once your safety is no longer threatened you should do a quick inventory on your entire body. When President Reagan was shot in 1981 he was unaware of it until he started having breathing problems. Even after his aide began to examine him, it was not immediately apparent that he had sustained a bullet wound. If you should find yourself in a similar situation it is obviously imperative you immediately seek medical assistance.

Leave the scene? One option is simply to leave the attackers where they lie and never look back. Reporting the incident to the police may bring complications into your life that you don't want or need. The preceding information is only to help make you aware of some of the choices you have. It is not legal or moral advice. The choices are up to you.

15
HOW TO PICK A
MARTIAL ARTS SCHOOL

The fact you've bought this book probably means you're interested in learning self-defense. Now that you've sampled some of the techniques in the preceding pages you may want to continue your martial arts education by enrolling in a school. Discussed here are some of the things you should consider when selecting a martial arts school.

STYLES

There's a bewildering assortment of martial arts styles to choose from. Generally they can be broken down into "hard" and "soft" styles, and styles that emphasize either kicks or hands.

Generally speaking, hard styles use movements that rely on power and strength, and soft styles use techniques that rely on being evasive and going "with the flow." For example, a hard style might block a punch and then hit, while a soft style's technique might be to step out of the way and then hit.

Which style you choose depends a lot on your body type and psychological make-up. If you are aggressive you may prefer a hard style such as Kempo Karate. If, on the other hand, you have a more relaxed, nonaggressive personality you may enjoy a style such as Tai Chi Kung-Fu.

"Kicking" styles such as Tai-Kwon-Do use a lot of kicking techniques, while Wing Chun Kung-Fu, for example, relies primarily on punching techniques. As with the hard/soft styles, which one you choose is a personal decision. It's a mistake to claim one style as superior to another. A woman with strong legs and a weak upper body may excel at Tai-Kwon-Do, but someone with a bad knee and strong arms may feel more comfortable with a punching style.

Another consideration when picking a style is how formal their traditions are. Some karate schools have very strict traditions that involve bowing to flags and never talking to instructors; other schools are extremely informal.

COST

How much will the lessons cost? This is an area requiring caution. Many schools are businesses first and martial arts schools second. Some schools try to get you to sign a long-term contract similar to many health clubs. I recommend you avoid this type of arrangement. Try to find a school in which you pay by the month; that way if you don't go you don't pay.

A local Kung-Fu school in Los Angeles charges sixty dollars a month and for that price you can attend classes whenever you want — even every night if you wish. Another Karate school in Los Angeles wants a deposit of five hundred dollars and expects you to sign up for a year (a total cost of about twelve hundred) — and you can only come to two classes a week. Both schools are run by well-known and respected instructors, so as you can see there's a wide range of options out there.

RANKS AND BELTS

Some styles and schools have extensive belt ranking systems. Generally Karate and Judo schools use belts as an indication of rank, but Kung-Fu schools don't.

Don't get fooled by a promise of rank. Some sales pitches involve comments such as, "you'll be a black belt within two years!" The rank means nothing—it's the amount of skill you will be taught that counts.

Forget about rank and belts. A mugger doesn't care about your "black belt," nor does a black belt magically make you invincible in a fight. Some styles in fact will give out a black belt to students who have never sparred!

SPARRING

Some schools don't have sparring sessions. Sparring means to actually fight another student while wearing protective equipment. Stay away from schools and instructors who don't allow sparring. Remember, *how you train is how you'll respond if you have to defend yourself.* You don't want your first sparring session to take place in the street! That's a lousy place to find out something doesn't work.

Some instructors claim that what they teach is too deadly to allow sparring. They're simply lying. A legitimate instructor will allow (and encourage) his student to spar under supervision. While it's true that some techniques can't be used in sparring, such as the side kick to the knee shown in this book, they can be "altered" so you can practice them. The side kick could be thrown to the upper thigh, for example, and be "pulled" before impact. If you run across a school in which everyone is walking around talking about how deadly they are, but nobody spars, ignore them and leave.

TEACHERS

You should check out a teacher's credentials since there are a lot of imposters out there. One way to do this is to give one of the martial arts magazines a call and ask if they know of the instructor and school. Most established martial arts instructors are well-known within the martial arts community. With a few phone calls you should be able to check them out.

Another way is to talk with some of the students at the school and see if they're happy with the classes. You should be allowed to watch a class, which will tell you a lot. Talk to some of the women in the class to see if there is discrimination toward women. Avoid instructors who feel women are "too weak" to learn self-defense.

EQUIPMENT

The best school I ever attended met in a small square room with a cold cement floor. It was a great school because the teacher *taught* lots of valuable lessons in each class. The only equipment used was a few hand-held bags and a training partner. On the other hand, one of the worst classes I ever attended took place in a carpeted plush environment, laden with all the latest equipment. It was lousy because the teacher didn't teach anything; he simply ran an army of students through endless exercises. When I tried to ask him some questions he yelled about the interruption.

If you want gym equipment, join a health club. You're signing up for self-defense lessons, not health club privileges.

INDEX

A

Advanced techniques, 173–93
Aftermath, 195–96
Air horns, 20
Alarm systems, 167–8
Ambulance, 195
Ankle stretch, 32
Appearance, 22–3
Arm around your shoulder, 125
Arm rolls, 30
Armlock, grabbed from behind with, 104–105
Armlock, rear, 103–104
Attackers, multiple, 173–82

B

Back, leg and arm stretch, 33
Back and leg stretch, 44
Back stretch, 43
Backfist, 73–4
Bear hug, front, 96–7
Bear hug, rear, 97–8
Behind, grabbed from, 98–100
Blocks, 76–8
Bridge, the, 48

C

Calf stretch, 39
Caliber of guns, 169–70
Car, in a, 133–4
Chair, standing on, 130
Close quarters, in, 111–22
Clothes, 15
Club, defending against a, 135–8
Crescent kick, 59–60, 90–1, 187–8
    spinning, 187–8

E

Elbow, horizontal, 70
Elbow, vertical, 71–2, 91–2
Elbow jab, 73
Elbow sandwich, 122
Environment, be aware of, 23
Equipment, 198

F

Face, grabbed by, 128–9
Fear, using, 20
Feints, using, 23–4, 87–8
    high, 87–8

First strike, 19
Flashlight, using as a weapon, 149–57
Front kick, 54, 81, 89–90
Front knee kick, 55
Front leg round kick, 61–2
Front punch, 67–9, 86, 87–90
Full thigh stretch, 42

G

Grabs you, when someone, 95–110
Ground, fighting from the, 191–3
Guns, 167–72
    being held at gunpoint, 171–2
    disadvantages of, 167–8
    holding an assailant at, 172
    tactics, 170–1
    types of, 168–9
    what caliber, 169–70
    what should you buy, 170

H

Hair, grabbed by, 108–9
Hand moves, basic, 67–80
Hands on your legs, 126–7
Hatchet kick, 186–7
Head roll and neck stretch, 27–9
Headlock, 103, 106–7, 189–90
    and throw, 189–90
    front, 103
Hip stretch, 46
Hit, where to, 24–5
    photos, 25
Hook kick, 60
Horizontal elbow, 70
Horns, air, 20

I

Injuries, 196
Inner leg stretch, 41
Inner thigh stretch, 36–7

J

Jab, elbow, 73
Jumping kick, 185

K

Karate chop, 74–6

Kicks, basic, 53–65
Kiss you, someone tries to, 121
Knee kick, front, 55
Knee kick, round, 61
Knife, defending against a, 138–48
Knife, using as a weapon, 158–62

L
Lawyer, 195
Learning self-defense, 13–7
Leg stretch, 40–1, 51
   advanced, 51
   inner, 41
Legs, hands on your, 126–7

M
Martial arts school, how to pick a, 197–8
Moving forward side kick, 57–9
Multiple attackers, 173–82

N
Noise, making, 20–1
Nonviolent solutions, 21–2

O
One arm take down, 183–5
Overconfidence, 16

P
Palm strike, 78–9, 84, 90–1
Phone booth, attacked in, 114–5
Police, 195
Power, achieving maximum, 79–80
Practice, 13–5
Punch, front, 67–9, 86, 87–9
Punch to the stomach, defense, 92–4
Push-ups, 38

R
Rear leg round kick, 62–3
Revolvers, 169
Ridge hand, 69–70, 89–90
Round kick, front leg, 61–2
Round kick, rear leg, 62–3
Round knee kick, 61
Runner's stretch, 49–50

S
Sandwich, elbow, 122
Semi-automatics, 169
Shotguns, 168
Shoulder, arm around, 125
Shoulder, grabbed by, 101–2
Shoulder and arm stretch, 31

Shoulder roll, 29
Side kick, 55–6, 57–9, 85
   moving forward, 57–9
Side sit-ups, 47
Side stretch, 35–6
Sitting down, 123–34
Sit-ups, 47–8
Sitting next to you, bothered by a man, 132–3
Slap block, 88–9
Sparring, 14, 198
Spin kick, 64, 82–3
Spinning crescent kick, 187–8
Stance, basic, 53
Standing on the chair, 130
Stomach stretch, 39
Straddle stretch, 42–3
Stranger tries to touch you, 131
Street, in the, 81–94
Stretching, 27–91
Strike, palm, 78–9, 84, 90–1

T
Tactics, 19–25
Teachers, 198
Thigh stretches, 36–7, 42
Throw, and headlock, 189–90
Touch you, stranger tries to, 131
Trouble, avoiding, 22–3
Types of guns, 168–9

U
Umbrella, using as a weapon, 162–6

V
Vertical elbow, 71–2, 91–2
Violence, 16–7

W
Waist stretch, 34–5, 45
Wall, back against, 116–20
Wall, pinned against, 115
Wall, pushed against, 111–3
Weapon, defending against a, 135–48
Weapons, using, 149–66
   flashlight, 149–57
   knife, 158–62
   umbrella, 162–6
Whistles, 20
Wing Chun kick, 65
Wing Chun Kung-Fu, 95
Woman, advantages of being, 19
Wrist, grabbed by one, 107–8
Wrist and forearm stretch, 37
Wrists, held by both, 109–10